Abortion and Ireland

David Ralph

Abortion and Ireland

How the 8th Was Overthrown

palgrave
macmillan

David Ralph
Department of Sociology
Trinity College Dublin
Dublin, Ireland

ISBN 978-3-030-58691-1   ISBN 978-3-030-58692-8   (eBook)
https://doi.org/10.1007/978-3-030-58692-8

Cover illustration: © John Rawsterne/patternhead.com

This Palgrave Pivot imprint is published by the registered company Springer Nature
Switzerland AG
The registered company address is: Gewerbestrasse 11, 6330 Cham, Switzerland

In memory of James Reid

ACKNOWLEDGEMENTS

The largest debt of gratitude is owed to each and every one of the women storytellers who courageously spoke out about their abortion histories in an effort to have the Eighth Amendment removed from the Irish Constitution. That Amendment was a regressive, misogynistic article inserted into the foundational document of the Irish State, and every Irish citizen alive now and in the future is better off that it is gone. Good riddance.

I would like to thank my colleagues in the Sociology Department at Trinity College Dublin. They provided useful feedback on some of the early ideas contained herein. I would also like to thank Mary Gilmartin and Jane Gray at Maynooth University for talking through the project with me. I am grateful too to Lynn Staeheli for her ongoing guidance and support of my academic work.

Thanks are also due to several friends whose good company and occasional wise words made the last year bearable. I'm thinking here of Killian Foley, Jules Hackett, Paddy Cahill, Paddy O' Dea, Mick Quinn, John Kerrigan, Irial Glynn, Jane O' Sullivan and James Hanrahan. I'm also thinking of Tony Tracy, Anne Reid, Luke Daly, Keith Elliot, Sarah O' Brien, Danny O' Brien, Paloma Viejo, Gavin Corbett, Simon Henderson, Conor McCaffery, Shane Perry, Andy Connolly and Jean-Thomas Arrigi de Cassanova.

Special thanks to Maria Judge, in whose house I started writing the first chapter of this book. Strangely, unexpectedly, but happily, I found myself writing the last chapter there too, and for this I am very grateful. Perhaps those middle chapters are missing something.

I must, before I forget, thank my family for their years of love and support. To my siblings Oliver, Siobhán and Mairéad, the in-laws Mick-Joe, Wayne and Grace, and the next generation Mikey, Ollie, Daíthí and Joanna, thank you all. Oh! And Paudie. Thank you too, Paudie. And my parents of course, Patsy and Josie, thank you thank you thank you.

CONTENTS

CHAPTER 1

Introduction

Abstract This chapter introduces the background to how the present study on the Repeal referendum arose. It charts some pivotal moments where the author encountered the subject of abortion at both an intellectual and personal level and how the author's curiosity around the subject came about. The chapter goes on to introduce the idea of how a culture of outspokenness on abortion began to develop in the Republic of Ireland in recent years. It discusses key events in this development, including the release of the Ryan Report into clerical child sex abuse in 2009, the implementation of savage austerity by the government in the early 2010s, and most crucially, the shocking and completely unnecessary death of Savita Halappanavar as a direct result of the existence of the Eighth Amendment.

Keywords Abortion · Sex education · Ryan Report ·
Eighth Amendment · Savita Halappanavar

On 25 May 2018, the Irish electorate went to the ballot box to decide in a referendum how it felt regarding a woman's right to choose what to do with a pregnancy. This was called the Repeal Referendum. The next day a huge crowd, which included myself and several of my friends, had thronged inside the courtyard of Dublin Castle to hear the announcement of the official result. The weather was sunny, the sky cloudless and blue.

© The Author(s) 2020
D. Ralph, *Abortion and Ireland*,
https://doi.org/10.1007/978-3-030-58692-8_1

A hush rippled through the expectant crowd when the returning officer Mr. Barry Ryan emerged onto the stage and neared the microphone. At approximately 3.30 p.m., Mr. Ryan read out the final tally of votes—and at that a deafening roar went up from those inside the castle's court-yard. It felt like the roar almost shook the courtyard walls, and instantly the atmosphere was that of a party. Some people started dancing. Others embraced. Some wept tears of joy, relief. Others chanted. One woman, I noticed, collapsed in contentment onto the centuries-worn cobbles.

The country, it was clear, had spoken in no uncertain terms: the pro-repeal Yes side had outvoted the anti-repeal No side two-to-one (Connor 2018). The implication now was that the Eighth Amendment of the Irish Constitution would be removed. That Amendment had criminalised abor-tion in almost all circumstances, meaning that those wanting to end an undesired, unchosen, or unviable pregnancy had to leave the jurisdiction for a termination, or, as they increasingly did in recent years, illegally order abortion pills online (Sheldon 2016).

Later, out on the streets, in the city's bars and restaurants, and later still in the nightclubs, the party continued as pro-Repeal supporters rejoiced in their hard-earned victory long into the small hours. A night like none other Dublin had ever witnessed.

In the days, weeks and months after the resounding 25 May refer-endum, there was a lot of discussion of the outcome (Abortion Rights Campaign 2019; Calkin 2020; Enright 2018; Mullally 2018; Scriven 2020). Pundits agreed: the vote was a historic one. Observers seemed to form a consensus: this result was of major import for contemporary Irish society. There was much talk of the end of old Ireland. There was much talk of the beginning of a new Ireland. The truth was probably somewhere in the middle.

In any event, the conclusion I drew from all this was that the refer-endum itself deserved close analytic attention. And so the immediate impetus behind this project sprang up in the direct aftermath of the 25 May 2018 vote.

But the seeds of it, I believe, actually took root years earlier, something I carried with me as a vague idea for a long time before it crystallised into a fully outlined, concrete book. Allow me to explain.

As far as I can remember my earliest encounter with the issue of abor-tion was in a philosophy class in university. This was the early 2000s, at National University of Ireland, Galway. I was eighteen, I was taking a first-year bioethics course, and about halfway through the second term the topic of abortion was up for discussion.

Prior to this, most of us were your typical Irish student, reserved, cards held tightly to our chests, fretful of speaking up in front of others. Issues like human cloning, animal rights, gene therapy, organ donation, assisted suicide—all these topics seemed to barely rouse the room, barely drew a glance up at the struggling lecturer.

Not so the week we covered abortion. This week the mood in the room was different. Now the class seemed to be charged, and it seemed to be split too, as those in favour of abortion loudly upbraided those opposed to it—and vice versa. I remember the lecturer, who was from England, had to intervene almost in the manner of a referee on a few occasions, and remind us that we were on a university campus and not a football pitch or a pub. I remember also that he seemed to be amused by us.

I was certainly surprised by the passion that had erupted all of a sudden in our previously sedate classroom. I didn't speak up that day, though I do remember finding myself more on the pro-choice side of the argument, if it was actual arguments—rather than bundles of sentiments—people presented. I wasn't entirely clear on what I thought about the whole subject of abortion, but I knew I didn't think, as some in the room screamed, that terminating a pregnancy was in every circumstance the moral equivalent of murdering an innocent baby.

As an adolescent in rural Ireland in the late 1990s, I'd had close to nothing by way of sex education either in school or at home. I suppose one legacy of growing up in what was still a dominant 'Catholic ethos' then in both my family and the community more broadly was to essentially throw a cloud of unknowing over most matters to do with the body, intimacy, desire, sex. Still, by the time I sat down in that university classroom to listen to the various pro- and anti-abortion positions of my fellow students, I knew I didn't want to become a teenage father. That much was clear. By then I'd experienced enough panicked incidents with my then-girlfriend: split condoms, late periods, occasional visits to occasionally judgemental doctors to ask for the morning-after pill. We barely knew what we were up to, fumbling, clutching, laughing; the culture, as it were, essentially forced us to figure things out for ourselves.

Yet we knew enough to know that life and the world weren't necessarily cast in two simple varieties of black and white. And during these panicked incidents, we talked. We talked about what we would do. We talked about what our options were. And we agreed. If my girlfriend had become pregnant and she had a child at this juncture in our young lives, it would probably spell the end of both of our third-level studies. We also agreed: what was not a probability but almost a certainty was that becoming parents then would have spelled a life of poverty for the foreseeable future. We had none of the magical thinking that seems to lay behind most pro-life arguments that everything related to do with having a child will just work out in the end. Ours, if you could call it such, was a sort of realist thinking around our parenting prospects at that time.

So, in the event of a pregnancy, we knew what we would do, no question. I'm not sure the language of intentional decision-making is even correct to describe this process, it was more an intuition, an instinct. There was little difficulty involved in these conversations either, little by way of breast beating.

That said, I do understand what people mean when they say that talking about abortion can be difficult. I can't imagine, for instance, getting into a conversation on the topic with my own mother. For reasons I can't, or maybe don't, want to pinpoint, it's just too strange, too uncanny.

But over the years there's been plenty of other people I've had private conversations with about abortion. I've had these conversations with male and female friends, with different girlfriends, sometimes with complete strangers. In this we were probably different to older generations, where abortion as a conversational topic was approached, if at all, in a highly coded language of euphemism, elision, silence.

These conversations with friends, partners, strangers have taken a familiar shape. Contraceptive failure. Or no contraception. A late period. Then a test. Then panic. Then a realisation that the principal actors are not long out of childhood themselves, that they're too young or too poor or too unprepared for parenthood. And in some cases, this has resulted in the pressing need for a woman I've known, in that classic Irish euphemism, 'to travel'.

Of these various abortion stories, there's one that stands out. A few years ago I became friends with a woman. I'll call her Clare. At some point, I don't recall exactly how, the subject of abortion came up. Clare told me her own abortion story. Or, as it turned out, her sort of abortion story.

Clare was twenty-six at the time, in a long-term relationship that was beginning to fray. For a range of reasons she was worried that her boyfriend wasn't going to make a suitable long-term partner. Around the same time she was having these worries, her period was late one month.

She waited, waited. But nothing.

She bought a pregnancy test. The result: blue.

She bought another pregnancy test. Again: blue.

What to do? Clare wondered. Could the relationship work out? Was it feasible at all to become a mother in these circumstances?

Clare told her boyfriend about the positive pregnancy tests. They agreed that the best thing to do would be to get an abortion. They made the arrangements, paid for the procedure. Clare told her family she was visiting a friend in London for the weekend. She flew out alone the night before; her boyfriend couldn't afford the trip.

Clare checked into a budget hotel close to the clinic. Once alone in the room she grew distressed. She really wasn't sure if she would go through with the procedure. The question, *Am I doing the right thing?* kept circling in her mind. She was from a strict Catholic background. Then she began feeling a sharp, searing pain in her abdomen. She thought the pain might be psychosomatic.

The pain grew worse. She went into the bathroom, she collapsed onto the floor. She had never experienced pain like this before. She clutched at her abdomen, she cried and cried, she screamed out in agony. The sounds coming out of her were more animal than human, she recalled.

Soon it became clear what was happening. There was nothing psychosomatic about the pain. Clare looked down between her legs. She was now bleeding heavily from her vagina. Over the next few hours she passed her pregnancy there on the bathroom floor of the budget hotel. She'd had a miscarriage.

The story shocked me. The story infuriated me. The whole incident just underlined how utterly benighted official Irish laws and health policies remained towards women's reproductive bodies and health.

This was the twenty-first century, after all. Ireland was supposed to be a civilised society, a decent society. And here was a young woman from that society bleeding and crying and scared for her life slumped over in a hotel bathroom in a foreign city, in a foreign country, having told none of her friends, none of her family what she was going through, not a solitary individual to give her any support.

Clare could have died right there and then on that bathroom floor. She was lucky she didn't.

Conversations like those with Clare and a number of others are, in part at least, what originally framed the idea for this book. However vaguely, the pages you are reading probably originated in all that talk, in all those stories.

Something else happened around this same time I was having these conversations. Someone—I'm almost sure it was my friend Tony—gave me a copy of Richard Yates' (1961) novel *Revolutionary Road*. I read, then immediately reread Yates' novel, which is set in the United States in 1955. Afterwards, I kept telling anyone who would listen that they had to read it.

On the surface, *Revolutionary Road* tells the story of a couple, Frank and April Wheeler. The Wheelers have an ideal-looking life, married, with a nice house in a nice new suburb in Connecticut. They have two beautiful children, and, materially, want for nothing with Frank's big job in New York City. Yet Frank and April are undergoing a spiritual crisis. They dream of dropping out from it all, moving to Paris to become … bohemians. Suburbia has become drab, a conservative world made just about bearable by excesses of alcohol, extramarital affairs and gossip.

Then April becomes pregnant for a third time. Then Frank has a change of heart. He no longer wants to go to Paris. Perhaps, despite all his talk, he never wanted to go at all. He's gotten a promotion now. He's also been having an affair with a considerably younger female colleague at work. He starts a charm offensive to convince April to stay in Connecticut, and continue the pregnancy. Frank's blandishments fail. April is adamant. She doesn't want another child. She wants to move to Paris. She's miserable with her life as a housewife. There are several domestic arguments. Frank claims to be disgusted by the idea of abortion. Finally, April agrees to stay, agrees to carry the child to term. But secretly she has planned to self-abort one day Frank is away at work. She buys the necessary implements. This is pre-Roe v Wade.

Revolutionary Road is a novel about many things. The gilded promises of youth. The disappointments of adult life. The fraught relations between men and women. The trials of marriage. The inevitability of loneliness.

Mostly, though, it is a blistering indictment of the brittleness and selfishness of the mid-twentieth-century American male ego. Nowhere is this better dramatised than in Frank's attempts to slyly coerce April into becoming a mother against her wishes for a third time. Frank pays a heavy price in the end for his self-involvement, for his attempts to control his wife, for his obsession with his male status. But April, the woman, the mother, pays a far heavier one. In the penultimate chapter, April dies on the bathroom floor from blood loss after her home abortion.

Revolutionary Road left a profound impression on me. Chief among these impressions was the link between a patriarchal social order and prohibiting abortion.

A short time later I moved back to Ireland from living abroad. This was late 2010. It was the height of EU-imposed austerity in the country. There had been swinging cuts to most public services. I was angry about the austerity. I was unemployed, and I was getting increasingly frustrated about being unemployed. This wasn't long after the Ryan Report was published either (Ryan Report 2009). The Ryan Report provided definitive evidence of the cruel, degrading treatment that children in Ireland's extensive network of Catholic church-run industrial schools had been subjected to. I was livid about this. The Ryan Report consists mostly of oral testimony from survivors, most of whom had suffered horrendous physical and sexual abuse at the hands of clerics.

For the first time in my life I started going on demonstrations. Flying placards, shouting slogans, demanding change.

Then, in November 2012, the terrible fate that befell Savita Halappanavar became public knowledge (Holland 2013). Savita Halappanavar, as I will discuss in detail in what follows, was an Indian dentist living in the West of Ireland when she presented at a maternity ward while miscarrying her pregnancy. Due to the Eighth Amendment, doctors were unable to intervene to help Ms. Halappanavar until the foetus died. By the time they did intervene it was too late. Ms. Halappanavar had developed septicaemia. She died of septic shock some days later.

This was the first real public scandal involving the Eighth Amendment that I had directly experienced in my adult life. I was shocked by the details that emerged about Savita Halappanavar's miscarriage. I was sickened by them. I went on demonstrations demanding the removal of the Eighth too. The pro-life claims that Ireland's laws on abortion vindicated the right to life of the 'unborn' just rang hollow to me. Especially when healthy young women were dying in our hospitals as a direct consequence of those laws.

I noticed something change after Savita Halappanavar's death. The change was slow at first, then it gathered pace. And what changed was that those private conversations around abortion that had been taking place for years took an outward turn. In particular, many women no longer felt saddled by stigma and shame that had long been associated with abortion. In some quarters, a culture of outspokenness on the subject of abortion began to develop. With alarm, more and more women realised that Savita's scandalous fate could be theirs. Their partners realised it too. Women, men, couples started talking abortion. But mostly women. And some publicly.

In the chapters that follow I detail this transformation in Ireland's abortion culture. In doing so I show how it had a direct bearing on the direction of the vote in May 2018 to allow women to decide whether and when they should have a child, or not.

References

Abortion Rights Campaign. (2016). *Submission to the citizens assembly*. Available at www.abortionrightscampaign.ie (accessed 1 June 2019).

Calkin, S. (2020). Abortion pills in Ireland and beyond: What can the 8th Amendment referendum tell us about the future of self-managed abortion? In K. Browne & S. Calkin (Eds.), *After repeal: Rethinking abortion politics* (pp. 73–89). London: Zed Books.

Connor, D. (2018). Savita Halappanavar's parents call for Yes vote. *RTE*. Available at https://www.rte.ie/news/eighth-amendment/2018/0520/964749-savita-halappanavar/ (accessed 22 June 2018).

Enright, A. (2018). Personal stories are precious things and they made the difference. *Irish Times*. Available at https://www.irishtimes.com/opinion/anne-enright-personal-stories-are-precious-things-and-they-made-the-differ ence-1.3510189 (accessed 28 May 2020).

Holland, K. (2013). *Savita: The tragedy that shook a nation*. Dublin: Transworld Ireland.

Mullally, U. (2018). Young women already being written out of the story of repeal. *Irish Times*. Available at https://www.irishtimes.com/opinion/una-mullally-young-women-already-being-written-out-of-the-story-of-repeal-1. 3516216 (accessed 28 May 2020).

Ryan Report. (2009). *The report of the commission to inquire into child abuse*. Dublin: Department of Children and Youth Affairs.

Scriven, R. (2020). Placing the Catholic Church: The moral landscape of repealing the 8th. In K. Browne & S. Calkin (Eds.), *After repeal: Rethinking abortion politics* (pp. 191–204). London: Zed Books.

Sheldon, S. (2016). How can a state control swallowing? The home use of abortion pills in Ireland. *Reproductive Health Matters, 24*(48), 90–101.

Yates, R. (1961). *Revolutionary road*. New York: Little Brown.

CHAPTER 2

A History of the Irish Abortion Debate

Abstract This chapter traces the history of elisions, euphemisms and silences that have characterised the Irish abortion debate historically. It opens by considering an extremely vocal, confessional contemporary incident involving two women who live-tweeted each step of an abortion journey from the Republic of Ireland to the United Kingdom in late 2016. Then the chapter continues by showing how the historical backdrop to such publicly shared accounts of abortion is almost the complete reverse insofar as for much of the country's independence, abortion occupied almost the status of a taboo in Irish public life. This is connected, the chapter argues, to the peculiar history of Irish sexuality, and the inordinate degree of influence the Catholic church exercised over matters to do with sex, the body and reproduction for most of the twentieth century. It shows further how this unhealthy clerical influence fell most heavily on the bodies of Irish women.

Keywords Abortion debate · Abortion silence · Catholic church · Sexuality · Fertility control

Introduction

On 20 August 2016, the Twitter handle #Twowomentravel began posting messages on the popular and much-used social media platform. The account was set up by two Irish women travelling from the Republic of

© The Author(s) 2020
D. Ralph, *Abortion and Ireland*,
https://doi.org/10.1007/978-3-030-58692-8_2

Ireland to a destination in the United Kingdom where one of the women was about to have a surgical abortion to end an unwanted pregnancy that day. Abortion at this point was still illegal in the Republic of Ireland. One of the opening Tweets from #Twowomentravel read: 'boarding, it's chilly. @endakennyTD' (Two Women Travel 2016a). The tweet was accompanied by a photograph of an early-morning airport, aircraft sitting on rain-sodden tarmac on the runway. The tweet and the photograph were directed to the Twitter account of Enda Kenny, the Irish Prime Minister at the time.

A follow-up tweet stated: 'We stand in solidarity with all women exiled @EndaKennyTD, his predecessors, his apologists' (Two Women Travel 2016b). Coming from a jurisdiction as the women did where abortion was then prohibited by law and carried the threat of a fourteen-year prison sentence, there was a real political audacity in mentioning the Prime Minister in their tweets.

Having arrived in the United Kingdom a photograph taken from the backseat of a black cab speeding along a motorway was posted by #twowomentravel alongside the text: 'pretty ordinary sights, in a place away from home, can't say it's comforting, though @endakennyTD' (Two Women Travel 2016c).

The next tweet stated, '@endakennyTD forced by more Irish in waiting room' (Two Women Travel 2016d), and alongside this text was an image of the dreary waiting room. There was cheap-looking furniture in the room, a television mounted on a wall showing a cycling race from the Olympics that were then taking place in Brazil, a table with a scatter of women's magazines including *Marie Claire*. Later on 20 August, above a photograph of a bland hotel twin-bedroom, #twowomentravel wrote: @endakennytd all done and dusted, we won't get home for another 24hrs' (Two Women Travel 2016e).

The following day, 21 August, the live-tweeting from the #twowomentravel account continued. The first tweet of the day read: posted, 'Not for the first or the last time a bleeding woman about to face a long treck home' (Two Women Travel 2016f), and the photograph here showed a faint bloodstain on the otherwise perfectly white coverlet of a hotel bed. Later, a photograph taken from the window of an airplane descending into Dublin airport was posted to the account with the accompanying text: 'We are nearly home. Thanks to everyone for unreal support – with one glaring exception. @endakennyTD' (Two Women Travel 2016g).

In total, the account #twowomentravel sent 28 tweets over a two-day period. By then it had 26,500 followers. The story of the women's journey was covered in all the Irish media as well as the Guardian and the BBC in the United Kingdom, and CNN in the United States (BBC 2016). The two women's purpose in setting up the account, as they claimed, was to showcase the sheer ordinariness of the journey—little more than 'a series of waiting rooms', 'a sequence of tediums' (Two Women Travel 2016h)—and one which an estimated twelve Irish women made on a daily basis to procure abortions in the United Kingdom. They hoped that by sharing their story publicly online they might put pressure on the government to implement long-overdue legal reform around abortion legislation in the Republic of Ireland.

A little over a year-and-a-half later, the women behind #twowomentravel had their hopes realised. The historic Repeal referendum held on 25 May 2018 passed by a landslide margin, with those in favour of Repeal outvoting those not in favour by an overwhelming two-to-one (Connor 2018). In the third highest turnout ever in an Irish referendum with 64.5 per cent of the electorate going to the ballot box, the people of the Republic had voted en masse to liberalise its abortion laws and make access to reproductive rights a reality for women living in the country (Kelly 2018). Pundits as well as pre-referendum polls had not predicted this scale of support, so the official result came as somewhat of a surprise. Only a week before polling day an Irish Times/IPSOS Mori poll found that just 44 per cent of voters intended to vote Yes, down five percentage points from the same poll carried out a month earlier in April, while a sizable 17 per cent stated they were as yet undecided (Waterson and Duncan 2018). When the final tally showed that over 66 per cent of voters had sided with the Yes campaign, celebrations erupted on the streets of the capital and in smaller towns and cities across the country. And in the major demographic areas of geography, gender and generation, again an enthusiastic majority in each backed the pro-choice position (Kelly 2018). Noting the relatively even spread of support for Repeal among not only liberal urban constituencies but also among rural constituencies, among men as well as women, and among younger as well as older voters, one commentator suggested that rather than the result being in any way divisive, it was in fact a 'fundamental rejection by the entire country of what has gone before' (Kelly 2018, para. 5).

Certainly when compared with the more liberal laws of the vast majority of its European neighbours, not only was the longevity but also the severity of Ireland's abortion ban a sort of anachronism by the late 2010s (Guttmacher Institute 2016). But how, it is worth asking, did the Irish electorate vote in such large numbers on 25 May that year to go down the road of legal abortion reform given that for the previous thirty-five years the county had one of the most restrictive abortion regimes in Europe?

The argument I develop here is that one answer to this question lies in endeavours much like those of #twowomentravel. By this I mean that a unique feature of the campaign to repeal the Eighth Amendment was that alongside traditional campaigning tactics such as street demonstrations, door-to-door canvassing, the distribution of pro-choice merchandise and so on, a key strategy of pro-choice advocacy groups was to encourage first-person abortion story-sharing by women in their efforts to convince voters of their position. The Eighth Amendment, introduced in 1983, effectively banned abortion provision in the country, and subsequently made discussing abortion publicly all but taboo (Harding 2014). This book shows how a remarkable normalising of abortion talk took place in the lead-up to the Repeal referendum, with women speaking publicly in unprecedented numbers and with unprecedented candour about their abortion histories.

In this, women storytellers like those behind #twowomentravel were mirroring the tactics of certain pro-choice movements in other contexts, where a new 'sound it loud, say it proud' narrative around abortion experiences has emerged in recent years as a central strategy in destigmatising abortion discourse. Or, as Arveda Kissling (2018) terms it, abortion activism and the sharing of abortion stories has shifted 'from a whisper to a shout'. Post-abortion, in most countries the norm for women remains self-censorship, concealment and non-disclosure of their history of terminating an unwanted pregnancy (Sanger 2017). In the Irish situation, this silencing has been particularly pronounced, with women's experiences long excluded from public debates on abortion. However, in the years preceding it and throughout the campaign to Repeal the Eighth, something changed. And what changed, principally, was that women found their voice. Or, put otherwise, pivotal to what De Zordo et al. (2016) call the shifting 'protest logics' of those seeking to liberalise the Irish reproductive rights regime were women with real experiences of the procedure. In this referendum, it was their voices and their publicly shared accounts of their abortion histories that were front and centre in defining the conversation. Throughout this book I detail the pivotal role played by personal abortion testimonies of women in achieving the stunning Repeal victory.

Before doing this, however, it is important also to chart what kind of 'abortion debate' preceded the emergence of this vocal activist tactic in attempting to liberalise Irish laws on pregnancy terminations. For the historical backdrop in the Republic of Ireland was a society wherein, until relatively recently, the topic of abortion had been all but muted (Fischer 2019). As a number of scholarly accounts have found, debating abortion has been a moral minefield, with the procedure shrouded in a public atmosphere of fear, stigma and shame (de Londras and Enright 2018; Earner-Byrne and Urquhart 2019; Fletcher 1995, 2001; Gilmartin and White 2011). Meanwhile, abortion talk—that is, women discussing their reproductive histories, including histories of abortion—was all but non-existent (Dully 2017; Rossiter 2009; Ruane 2000). Since abortion was illegal in the Republic of Ireland, those who travelled overseas to access abortion services, mostly in the United Kingdom, trailed a burden of secrecy, lies and subterfuge in their wake (Quesney 2015). Not only did few ever publicly discuss their abortion journeys for fear of the social opprobrium such disclosure might provoke—few ever even disclosed their abortion histories to anyone beyond a select band of confidantes. The social environment around abortion in the country was, in a word, hostile. As Ruane (2000, 6) put it, 'Irish society needs women's silence to keep its good opinion of itself', while almost a decade later Rossiter (2009, 11), in her investigation into Irish abortion seekers in the United Kingdom, stated that 'we still wait to hear them speak out in their own name'.

The history of this particular silence is intimately connected, I show in the remainder of this chapter, to the politics of reproductive governance in independent Ireland. As such, Irish life has been characterised by a deeply pro-natalist state that often relegated women to the status of second-class citizens whose only legitimate place in society was that of mothers within the marital home (Smyth 1998, 2005). Promoted by dogmatic Catholic teachings on the body and sex, a highly conservative moral climate surrounding sexuality in general but female sexuality in particular came to dominate for much of the twentieth century (Farrell 2012; Hill 2003; Hug 1999; McAvoy 1999, 2012a). Everyday issues to do with sexual intimacy, pregnancy, birth, fertility control and, of course, abortion were all controlled by the restrictive interventions of a highly authoritarian state/church apparatus (Speed 1992). Anyone deviating from the idealised standards of normative sexual conduct laid down primarily by the church were dealt with severely, often facing incarceration, ostracism or exile (O'Sullivan and O'Donnell 2012). This, as the next section shows, was particularly the case in the treatment to single women who gave birth to children outside of matrimony. In relation to abortion, long before social media sensations like that of #twowomentravel went 'viral', an understandable reticence persisted on the subject. The lived realities of the thousands of Irish women who each year either travelled abroad for a termination or somehow procured one in the state largely went unheard, unrecorded (Oaks 2002). In fact, as the following sections detail, in most decades since independence any efforts to speak out around what was a highly criminalised procedure went ignored, and anything resembling an 'abortion debate' took place within the strictures of a Catholic morality that rarely referred to medicine when discussing best practice in obstetrics, and almost never took women's own experiences into account (de Londras and Graham 2013).

A Brief History of Irish Sexuality

In an article from over twenty years ago, Tom Inglis (1997, 7) could rightly claim that 'sociological analysis of Irish sexuality has been notable for its absence'. It is fair to say that Inglis's statement no longer holds so true. In the intervening two decades, a great deal of further insight has been provided on the subject of sex in Ireland, none less than by Inglis himself, one of the pioneering scholars of the sociological analysis of Irish sexuality (see Inglis 1997, 1998a, b, c, 2005, 2014).

In his research Inglis largely adopts a Foucauldian approach, examining how discourses around the body, sex and reproduction articulated by the state/church nexus sought to police sexuality in the nascent Irish Republic from the 1920s onwards. Inglis (1998a) argues that because of the Catholic church's stranglehold over education and health care, it was the church hierarchy who enjoyed a 'moral monopoly' over discussions of the sexual arena, and in this they received state support and endorsement. As Kitchin and Lysaght (2004, 87) state, 'Given the strong links between State and Church in Ireland, with the church running schools and social welfare, Catholic civilising of the body was state-sponsored'.

In this context, then, church dogma cast sexuality not simply as a matter of biological reproduction but also, crucially, as a matter of social morality (Fischer 2017). The church, through its extensive network of institutions and agents (priests, nuns, Catholic educated teachers,

Catholic educated doctors, nurses, midwifes) strictly defined, as Inglis (1997, 5) put it, 'a classification of who could do what to whom, when, where and how' around sex. Simply, sexual rectitude was defined entirely by monogamous, procreational sex between a married man and a married woman (Hilliard 2000). Debate about sexual pleasure and recreational over reproductive sex was censored in public life, with all references to sex from the pulpit to the parliament to the classroom almost exclusively framed within a 'thematic of sin' (Inglis 1998b). Contraception and abortion were criminalised, divorce was forbidden. Individuals and groups who deviated or transgressed from the narrowly conceived rules of sexual respectability—unmarried mothers, prostitutes, non-celibate bachelors, homosexual men, lesbians—were in many cases incarcerated in homes, asylums and prisons, and in every case they were 'branded as sinners'.

Inglis and others (see in particular Ferriter's [2009] encyclopaedic account of the history of Irish sexuality) emphasise that in reality the Irish may not have been necessarily any more chaste, pure or virginal than people in any other nation in relation to their sexual conduct. Indeed, recent revelations about the extent of clerical child sex abuse, paedophilia, incest and rape within families, as well the high levels of prostitution, venereal disease and infanticide shows that the Irish history of sexuality is by no means a history of sexual innocence (Rattigan 2012). Inglis (2014) sums up the rank hypocrisy of the church position on sexuality, stating bluntly that for much of the time the clergy enjoyed this moral stranglehold over its flock, many priests and bishops were known to have had sex *and* children, while many others were known to have had sex *with* children. But what was distinctive about Irish sexual life was the scale of power wielded for much of the twentieth century by Church authorities to deem who was sexually saved, who sexually damned (Ferriter 2009). Or as Inglis (1998c) phrases it, the 'moral monopoly' enjoyed by clerical figures in Ireland around sex may be unprecedented in contrast to other countries in Europe, giving them a disproportionate influence in delineating sexual morality, and, as importantly, sexual immorality.

A number of scholars have detailed how this particularly rigid form of Catholicism in Ireland fused with an emergent twentieth-century nationalism to produce an especially toxic view of sexuality (Ferriter 2009; Hilliard 2003; Smyth 2005). From 1922 onwards, the newly independent postcolonial Irish Free State, as it was then called, sought desperately to distinguish itself from its former coloniser (Fischer 2019). Besting the

British militarily or economically was clearly not possible, so one arena where the Irish might affirm their superiority was that connected to social morals and virtue. Accordingly, the church, supported by the state, set about cultivating a morally upstanding and righteous people in contrast to the supposed moral vice and licentiousness widespread across British society (McAvoy 1999).

Yet the burden of upholding this national moral purity fell uneven on the bodies of Irish men and Irish women, with the latter seen as the ultimate guardians of the nation's virtue (McAuliffe 2009). A particular ideal of Irish maidenhood and sexual honour came to dominate in this particular sexual imaginary, whereby devoted married motherhood was the only avenue available to women as sexual beings (Earner-Byrne 2007). This positioning of women as committed domestic figures was ensconced in the 1937 Constitution, with Article 42.1.2 stating, 'In particular, the State recognises that by her life within the home, woman gives to the state a support without which the common good cannot be achieved' (Constitution of Ireland 1937).

Any woman not living up to this ideal, not contributing to the 'common good', was considered socially and morally problematic. As Fischer (2016, 833) states, 'the moral purity at stake in the project of Irish identity formation was essentially a sexual purity enacted and problematized through women's bodies'. In particular, women engaged in sexual activity outside of matrimony and who gave birth to 'illegitimate' children were deemed a threat to this fledgling project of nation-building (Hogan 2020). A discourse of 'shame' was mobilised by church leaders and conservative laypeople in order to cast aspersions on such women, whose impure bodies potentially undermined the foundations of national virtue (Crowley and Kitchin 2008).

In many instances these stigmatised women either emigrated, mostly to Britain, or if they remained in Ireland were often incarcerated in religious-run intuitions where their supposedly sullied, blemished bodies could be hidden away from public view (Cox 2009). The Magdalene Laundries confined many such 'polluted' women, and as Fischer (2016, 835) argues, the nature of the work carried out in these institutions was highly symbolic, too: the act of becoming pregnant outside of wedlock, engaging in unsanctioned sexual activity, was 'read as stains upon their very characters and bodies, stains that could be removed (though never quite) through repentance and the backbreaking work of washing away stains from dirty laundry'.

This highly gendered, sexualized shaming of certain female bodies has certainly loosened in recent times (Bacik 2004). The church's reformatory institutions such as its mother and baby homes, laundries and industrial schools have all but been closed down, and a general climate of tolerance and greater openness prevails in matters of intimacy and sex (Crowley 2013). More recently, historians, feminists and others have charted how the hegemony of Catholic teachings around sexuality and the shaming of women's bodies has been successfully challenged by various social groups since the 1970s onwards (Connolly 2002; Daly 2016; Finnegan 2004). Resistance to Catholic conservatism initially came from women advocates demanding access to contraception (which will be discussed in more detail in the next section). Later, the challenge was taken up by gay and lesbian groups to decriminalise homosexuality. And while they have been bitterly contested, referenda have been passed by the Irish electorate in recent decades taking divorce and homosexuality off the statute books (Fahey and Layte 2007). In general, scholars agree that as church membership and active participation in the Catholic church has decreased, a significant shift has taken place away from the Catholic disciplining of sexuality that long shrouded the act in secrecy, shame and stigma. This has resulted in almost a sea-change in attitudes towards sex, with a much more secular, liberal focus on sexual diversity, preference and freedom now prevailing (Canavan 2012).

In effect, many of the sexual mores commonplace in other Western countries have belatedly but definitively entered into Irish society and Irish sexual life, with many younger cohorts often incredulous at the sexual prudery and morality of older generations (Crowley 2013). Such has been the social revolution around sex and sexuality in Ireland that in 2015 the country became the first in the world to pass by popular vote new legalisation sanctioning gay marriage (Healy et al. 2015). This was a sharp turnabout for a country that only decriminalised same-sex sexual activity in 1993, and only then after being compelled to by the European Court of Human Rights (Bacik 2004). That was in the same year that the full ban on the sale of condoms in public outlets was finally lifted (Earner-Byrne and Urquhart 2019). The last of the religiously run mother and baby homes finally closed its doors in 1996 (McCarthy 2010).

So it is fair to say that a significant and relatively rapid loosening of norms with regard to sexuality has been witnessed in Irish society of late. Yet one particular domain where the country markedly failed to converge with the majority of its European neighbours was the issue of abortion and reproductive rights for women. The church's moral conservatism and its long-standing disciplining of female sexuality continued in many ways to hold sway when it came to the issue of women's bodily autonomy in determining their reproductive destinies (Porter 1996). In the next section, I detail the history of fertility control operational in independent Ireland, with particular focus on the lead-up to the 1983 referendum on abortion that ultimately inserted the Eighth Amendment into the Constitution.

A Brief History of Irish Fertility Control Until the Eighth Amendment

Given this climate of moral intransigence that governed sexuality, and in particular women's sexuality, it is little surprise that abortion in independent Ireland was prohibited by law (Barry 1988). Of course, in this Ireland was little different than many other states. Reproduction is central to all nation-building processes (Solinger 2005). In most political communities both historical and contemporary, state interventions in the form of pro-natalist measures have tried to encourage particular modes of reproduction, or tried to suppress others through various anti-natalist measures (Kligman 1998; Luibheid 2013). To this end, abortion regulation is crucial for enforcing, as Calkin (2019) has it, prevailing norms of patriarchy, heterosexuality, citizenship and motherhood. Following a biopolitical turn in population governance across Europe and North America, Ireland was by no means unusual, then, in criminalising abortion as a way of controlling its people, and in particular its women (Fischer 2019). What was unique about the Irish situation, however, was the degree of antipathy not only towards abortion but also towards all other forms of birth control (Girvin 2018). In this section I show how, overseen by a deeply dogmatic Catholic moral order on sex, the Irish state moved in the opposing direction to most of its neighbours throughout the latter half of the twentieth century in relation to women's reproductive rights. This culminated in 1983 when a pro-life lobby group successfully agitated for a clause to be inserted in the Irish Constitution to protect the life of the 'unborn', thus making Ireland's already restrictive abortion laws even more so (Beatty 2013). Interestingly, at this same time progressive waves of reform around abortion provision were sweeping across many neighbouring European countries, including Catholic Europe (Wanrooij 1999).

After the foundation of the state in 1922, the 1861 Offences Against the Person Act that criminalised any woman who obtained or attempted to obtain an abortion remained in situ (Fox and Murphy 1992). In 1929 Britain introduced the Infant Life Act, which allowed provisions to be made for therapeutic or medical abortions in cases where a woman's life was endangered by her pregnancy (Earner-Byrne and Urquhart 2019). A similar law, however, was not enacted in the new Irish state, and in that same year the Irish Free State introduced the Censorship Act, prohibiting the distribution of all printed material advocating the 'unnatural prevention of conception' (McAvoy 2012b).

Six years later, in 1935, the Amended Criminal Act banned the importation and sale of all contraceptives (Girvin 2008). All matters to do with fertility control were framed within a language of morality over and above that of medicine (or rights). And from the pulpit to the parliament, authority figures viewed artificial birth control more often than not as a gateway to abortion and promiscuity rather than something that might be integral to women's health (Hill 2003; Kelly 2020). A 1969 Papal encyclical titled *Humanae Vitae* reaffirmed the continuing unequivocal Catholic ban on abortion, contraception and divorce as central to Catholic teachings (Foley 2019). To the disappointment of fledgling feminist and liberal sectors of society, the message of *Humanae Vitae* was enthusiastically endorsed by the church hierarchy in Ireland, and even *coitus interruptus*, the withdrawal method, was still being denounced in various church pastorals as late as the 1970s as a mortal sin (Daly 2016; Holohan 2018; McGarry 2018).

With such a prohibitive regime around family planning and fertility in operation in the Republic for much of the twentieth century, most women accepted this reality, becoming pregnant year on year, giving birth to child after child once married (Earner-Byrne 2007). Some were doubtlessly happy to do this too, helping the burgeoning Catholic state cultivate its self-image of moral superiority over other nations, primarily its nearest neighbour Britain. Others, however, were less content with this situation. And on occasion this resulted in some women resorting to certain informal, illegal methods to regain a degree of freedom over their reproductive bodies (Delay 2018). As Plummer (2010, 167) argues, even within the most hegemonic socio-sexual orders, there are always 'sexual subterranean traditions' which, he states, 'run against the grain, where any ideas of a dominant world … are subverted, resisted, quietly ignored, or loudly challenged'.

Testimony to these efforts at resistance to the inflexible Catholic sexual order of the time were the high incidence before the courts in the 1940s and 1950s of cases of postnatal infanticide, birth concealment, child abandonment, self-harm to end a pregnancy, as well as, of course, 'back-street' abortions (Rattigan 2008, 2012). Historical research has shown that in the first half of the twentieth century the numbers of Irish women, some married with children, some single, who attempted to self-abort with pills, potions and other remedies was especially high prior to the passing of the 1967 Abortion Act in the United Kingdom (Rose 1978). At the same time, a sort of underground network of 'handywomen'— that is, self-trained abortionists—alongside sympathetic midwives, nurses and pharmacists developed, whereby a woman would be assisted through a variety of means to, in one of the euphemisms of the time for abortion, 'bring on' menstruation (Daly 2006; McAvoy 2004). Once abortion became legal in Britain in 1967, this, as Earner-Byrne and Urquhart (2019, 69) put it, 'revolutionised the options open to women on the island of Ireland who could and did travel to avail of legal and safe abortions'.

In fact, all of this suggests that the status quo was not quite so dominant as might be imagined throughout the 1950s and 1960s. Certainly in decades to come this dominance was to be challenged in a much more public fashion, especially around the issue of contraception (Enright and Cloatre 2018). Or, put differently, some of the 'subterranean traditions' that were latent were about to rise to the surface. Of note here was how a younger generation in the late 1960s and early 1970s who had been exposed to ideas of sexual autonomy and the notion that religion should have only a limited influence on private and family life were adopting a more secular, liberal outlook compared to previous generations (Daly 2016). As part of this, they were articulating dissatisfaction that clerics continued to be moral arbiters in matters related to sex and the body (Arnold 2009). Many were keenly aware, too, of the extraordinary hypocrisy of a nation whose claims to moral absolutism could only be maintained by indulging in the fiction that, in another popular euphemism, the 'boat to Liverpool' from 1967 onwards was not a mundane reality for many Irish women who found themselves unwillingly pregnant (Bloomer and O'Dowd 2014).

A nascent women's movement in the 1970s was a major plank of this liberalising force in Irish society (Connolly 2002). And one of the key early demands of groups like the Irish Women's Liberation Movement,

Irishwomen United, the Well Woman Centre, the Irish Family Planning Association and the Contraceptive Action Campaign was for legislation to be passed lifting the blanket ban on contraception (Stopper 2005). Their efforts, which included street demonstrations and other direction action tactics, received a major boost after a 1974 Supreme Court ruling that found that married couples had a right to make private decisions regarding family planning (Muldowney 2015). The case before the Supreme Court involved Mary McGee, a married mother of four who had had a stroke while pregnant and had been advised by her doctor to avoid future pregnancies. Mrs. McGee tried importing condoms from overseas but customs confiscated them under the provisions of the 1935 Criminal Law Amendment Act that banned all contraceptives. In the wake of the McGee ruling, legislation was introduced at last three years later under the Health Act 1979 (de Londras and Enright 2018).

But this legislation was a compromise at best. It only partially liberalised the law around contraceptive access, with condoms, the pill and other prophylactics now available for the first time since 1935 to married couples only, and only from a doctor under prescription for so-called 'bona fide family planning' purposes (Girvin 2018). There was evidence, too, that well into the 1980s many pharmacists in rural areas refused to stock any form of contraceptives regardless of the new legislation (Kelly 2020). However, as has been noted by a number of legal scholars, progress had certainly been made, taking contraception out of the hands of the state and recasting it as a private matter between married couples (Fletcher 1998, 2001, 2018; Harding 2014; Mullally 2008). Significant, too, was that the Health Act 1979 shifted control of contraception away from the remit of the Department of Justice towards the Department of Health, thus beginning the process of medicalising the issue of birth control rather than criminalising it (Smyth 2015).

Yet this modest liberalisation around birth control was to be met by a serious backlash. Led by certain right-wing politicians, segments of the Catholic hierarchy, as well as some prominent members of the medical establishment, in the early 1980s conservative forces mobilised to prevent what they saw as any further liberal encroachments on the upstanding Catholic sexual culture of the nation (O'Reilly 1997). One popular figure of the period, Bishop Kevin McNamara, lamented what he termed the spread of the 'contraceptive mentality', blaming it for a host of social ills including undermining the status of the family in Irish life (Beatty 2013).

These organisational efforts resulted in the formation of the Pro-Life Amendment Campaign (PLAC), a lobby group launched in 1981 determined to insert a clause into the Constitution that would place the right to life of the 'unborn' on an equal constitutional footing as that of the pregnant woman (Fletcher 1998). The emergence of PLAC was unusual, for there was little debate in the country at the time about legislating for abortion, which was already illegal under the 1861 Offences Against the Person Act (Earner-Byrne and Urquhart 2019). Some have argued that privacy rulings like the 1973 Roe v Wade in the United States and the 1976 McGee ruling by the Irish Supreme Court alarmed anti-abortionists into proposing the amendment over fears that abortion too would become a matter of privacy (Francome 1992). Others have suggested that abortion was one of the more dramatic chapters in Ireland's ongoing 'culture wars', as a constituency of traditional, older, rural voters grew increasingly troubled at the gains being made by feminists and liberals in Irish society throughout the 1970s (Hug 1999). Others still have argued that abortion was a key trope in the postcolonial ideology of independent Ireland, as the Irish state grew more and more 'pro-life' in its efforts to distinguish itself from its increasingly 'pro-choice' former coloniser Britain (Fletcher 2001). One pro-life campaigning poster from the period certainly captured this postcolonial mentality, declaring: 'The abortion mills of England grind Irish babies into blood that cries out to heaven for vengeance' (cited in Earner-Byrne and Urquhart 2019, 77).

Whatever the precise motives behind the emergence of PLAC, what is clear is that the proposal this organisation tabled to amend the Constitution created one of the most divisive, vicious atmospheres in Irish public life for months in advance of polling day on 7 September 1983 (Muldowney 2013). The proposed amendment read: 'The State acknowledged the right to life of the unborn, and with due regard to the equal right to life of the mother, guarantees in its laws to respect, and, as far as practicable, by its laws to defend and vindicate that right' (cited in Citizens Assembly 2017, 5). Such was the level of animosity between pro- and anti-amendment groups that the *Irish Times* memorably described the campaign as 'the second partitioning of Ireland' (Hesketh 1990).

In hindsight many of the criticisms made of the amendment now read like prophecies. Primary here was how the life of the mother and the life of the unborn foetus were to be placed on an equal constitutional footing. This, several argued, including the Attorney General of the time, would inevitably create a 'chilling' effect on doctors when dealing with difficult pregnancies (Muldowney 2015). As a doctor now had to display equal regard for the life of the unborn baby, any room for legal manoeuvre to protect the life of seriously ill pregnant women would be restricted. It was suggested that women's health would inevitably be compromised if the amendment passed, leading to delays in providing potentially life-saving interventions to desperately sick pregnant women (Smyth 1995). Despite these arguments, the Amendment passed, with 66.9 per cent of voters in favour (Schweppe 2008). As has been well documented, since the introduction of the Eighth Amendment, all of the dangers foreseen to maternal health by enshrining the life of unborn babies in the Constitution came to pass on numerous, numerous occasions over the next thirty-five years (Mullally 2018).

A Brief History of Irish Fertility Control After the Eighth Amendment

The Amendment passed and the main pro-life players celebrated their victory and the strengthened ban on abortion. However, Lindsey Earner-Byrne and Diane Urquhart (2019) in their comprehensive *The Irish Abortion Journey, 1920–2018* convincingly argue that the insertion of the Eighth into the Constitution may, ultimately, have been a false victory for those opposed to abortion in Ireland. For what the campaign on the Eighth decisively did do was to turn abortion into a potent political issue (Earner-Byrne and Urquhart 2019). Up until the formation of the PLAC and their aggressive, outspoken pro-life campaign, the subject of abortion was rarely aired in Irish public life (O'Connor 1992). Now, after a three-year public conversation on abortion provision in advance of the vote, it was permanently on the agenda.

Interestingly, a 1984 survey by the European Value Systems Study found that the ground was shifting in terms of attitudes towards abortion (Fogarty et al. 1984). Prevalent among the general population was widespread antipathy to abortion. However, and this was crucial, a majority of those under forty-five believed that therapeutic abortions were justified to protect a woman's health (Fogarty et al. 1984). The Eighth, argue Earner-Byrne and Urquhart (2019, 81), had 'stirred up as much as it settled'.

One topic which now received much more attention from journalists and others in the aftermath of the Eighth was the moral hypocrisy of a nation with a proud pro-life self-image that relied for this self-image on Irish women secretly and silently travelling in the thousands each year to Britain to end unwanted, unviable or dangerous pregnancies (Jackson 1987). Another incident that exposed the cruel underside to much Catholic social teaching on sexuality was the case of Anne Lovett (Maguire 2001). Lovett, a schoolgirl aged fifteen was heavily pregnant when she wandered into the grotto of a Catholic church in late January 1984 in Granard, Co Longford. There, and all alone, she gave birth in the grotto grounds beneath a statue of the Virgin Mary, but both she and her baby died of exposure during the night. The story was a media sensation, and there were public outpourings of grief for the teenager (Solomons 1992). The case, many argued, highlighted that Ireland was not a country in any way compassionate towards women or girls who found themselves unwillingly pregnant (Muldowney 2013). In fact, the tragic fate of Anne Lovett showed that it remained deeply punitive and unkind (McCafferty 1985).

Five years after the Eighth, matters were to get even worse for women wanting to end a pregnancy. In 1988 the Supreme Court ruled that providing information to pregnant woman about abortion services outside the jurisdiction was also an infraction on the right to life of the unborn (Fletcher 1998). In practical terms this meant that it was now a crime for pregnancy counselling services, doctors or anyone else to refer patients to abortion clinics in the United Kingdom or elsewhere. After the ruling, British magazines on sale in Ireland had advertisements for abortion services in the United Kingdom censored (Ferriter 2009). An underground network of support organisations developed to assist women with making arrangements for terminations overseas, and phone numbers of abortion clinics in Britain were found scribbled on the walls of female public toilets all across the country (Earner-Byrne and Urquhart 2019). But despite these efforts at circumventing the new law, the overall impact of the information blackout was to create a general atmosphere of fear and intimidation for women seeking abortions (Randall 1992). This mood was further heightened in 1991 when the Irish government successfully inserted a protocol into the Maastricht Treaty that prevented the European Community from interfering in the Irish laws on abortion (O'Toole 2003).

And then, in 1992, the X Case happened, and the political heat around the subject of abortion skyrocketed once more (Smyth 1995). The X Case involved a fourteen-year-old girl who had conceived a child as a result of rape by a family friend and was subsequently injuncted by the Attorney General from travelling to the United Kingdom to abort her pregnancy (Mullally 2018). In what came to be seen as one of the more egregious examples of the constitutionally imposed cruelty of the 1983 amendment, it was only when the Supreme Court intervened that the teenager was granted the right to leave the jurisdiction for an abortion because of a risk to her life by suicide (Gilmartin and White 2011). The case received blanket coverage in the media at the time. Angry demonstrations took place across Dublin throughout the court hearings, with outraged protestors comparing the country to an internment camp for pregnant young women (Earner-Byrne and Urquhart 2019). The Supreme Court now ruled that a woman had a right to an abortion under the Eighth Amendment if there was a real and substantial risk to her life from the pregnancy, including on the grounds of suicide (Bacik 2015).

In the wake of the X Case, the government ran three abortion-related referenda in late 1992. The Thirteenth Amendment to the Constitution passed, which granted women the right to travel for abortion services overseas (O'Carroll 2012). The Fourteenth Amendment also passed, which granted women the right to access information on abortion services outside the jurisdiction (O'Carroll 2012). However, the substantive issue as it was called, the Twelfth Amendment, failed to pass, which was an attempt by the government to reverse the ruling of the Supreme Court in relation to the X Case (O'Carroll 2012). In its own wording, this amendment stated that 'the risk of self-destruction' of a mother was not sufficient legal ground for a termination. Despite the Twelfth being rejected by the Irish people, no legislation followed to enact the Supreme Court ruling on the X Case (Holland 2013). In fact, six successive Irish governments failed to legislate for this, leaving a legislative vacuum around abortion provision in the state. A similar referendum ran in 2002 also attempted to subvert the 1992 Supreme Court ruling, but again this failed to pass with the Irish people voting for a second time to permit abortion in cases where a mother's life was at risk as a result of suicidality (de Londras and Enright 2018).

But despite holding five referenda in under twenty years on the issue, none of this did anything to stem the flow of women travelling between the Republic and mostly the United Kingdom for terminations throughout the 1980s and 1990s (Stopper 2005). And despite the seemingly interminable legal wrangling over the rights of 'unborn children' versus those of pregnant women, rarely during all this time were the voices of the actual women behind the abortion journeys ever heard from (Healey 2008). Or, as Ruane (2000, 4) put it, 'theological and legal argument supplant the personal testimony of women'.

Mary Holland, a prominent Irish journalist throughout the 1980s and 1990s, was an exception to this. In 1983 she wrote about her own abortion (and subsequently received much hate mail from anti-abortionists) (Ferriter 2014). Twelve years later, in 1995, she returned to the subject in the aftermath of the X case, lamenting the ongoing lack of any female voices in the public domain describing their abortion experience. She wrote, 'It would be an enormous relief if some younger woman or women were to start writing about the issue of abortion from personal experience and leave me to the relatively easy task of analysing the peace process. Please' (cited in Ferriter 2014, para. 12). Her pleas went unheeded. Instead, as has been found in several studies, a general climate of stigma and shame surrounding abortion promoted by the country's vocal pro-life lobby intimidated women with experience of terminations into keeping their stories private for the most part (Bloomer and O'Dowd 2014; Connolly 2002; Kennedy 2001).

One now-notorious example of how such stories failed to reach the Irish public occurred in 1994 when a documentary called *50,000 Secret Journeys* was axed from airing on 29 March that year (Siggins 2016). RTE, the national broadcaster, had commissioned director Hilary Dully to make *50,000 Secret Journeys*, a film about the women who had travelled to the United Kingdom for pregnancy terminations, estimated at that time to be roughly 50,000. When *50,000 Secret Journeys* was finally screened over seven months later on 27 October, first it was moved away from its initial prime-time billing and included as part of a late-night current affairs package. Then the interviews with the three Irish women who had had abortions in the United Kingdom that made up the bulk of the original footage had been removed entirely from the final edit and were replaced with contributions from a barrister, a social worker, and an academic. And finally, the documentary had also been renamed *The Abortion Debate*. Dully's initial aim, she explained, was precisely to avoid this type of documentary format whereby expert analysis is favoured over the voices of those who have actually lived through the experience under consideration (Siggins 2016). Dully was informed by RTE executives that the edit was necessary to achieve 'balance' and 'objectivity' on the abortion issue. In Dully's view, however, what this merely functioned to do was 'disempower and marginalize the experiential narrative' (cited in Siggins 2016, para. 14).

This disempowering, this marginalising of Irish women's abortion experience did, however, finally begin to change somewhat in the late 1990s, early 2000s. For one, the topic started receiving much more media coverage, mainly by female journalists interested in the impact of Ireland's increasingly out-of-step abortion regime (McAvoy 2008). Then in 2000, a study by the Irish Family Planning Association titled *The Irish Journey: Women's Abortion Stories* was published (Ruane 2000). This was groundbreaking in that it represented the first full-length volume giving a voice to the women behind the statistics of approximately 5000 abortion journeys made each year to the United Kingdom. One contributor made the astute observation, 'If it was the numbers that counted, we would surely be viewed as normal as the girl next door' (Ruane 2000, 13). Another pioneering study came in 2009, with the publication of Ann Rossiter's *Ireland's Hidden Diaspora: The Abortion Trail and the Making of a London-Irish Underground, 1980–2000*. This book helped to further disrupt the silence that had settled around Ireland's abortion regime by allowing women forced into travelling to the United Kingdom for terminations to speak out in their own words (though at this point few were yet to spoke out in their own name). As importantly, Rossiter (2009) also shed light on the informal, sometimes clandestine, networks of women-led support groups that arose between Britain and Ireland to assist Irish women seeking abortions throughout recent decades.

In effect, what accounts like these were beginning to do was to bring the 'subterranean traditions' that had long existed around Irish abortion seekers to the surface, to finally 'run against the grain' of official Ireland's proud but increasingly untenable pro-life policy stance (Plummer 2010, 168). And what these stories showed was that being forced to travel to procure an abortion outside the state was, in fact, something deeply traumatising for many women, something deeply stigmatising (Ryan 2007). As abortion remained criminalised in Ireland, most obtained their terminations under a cloud of secrecy, subterfuge, and shame, both before and long after the procedure (Sheldon 2018). Most, too, felt extremely isolated throughout the entire process, unable in some cases to ever tell family and friends about their experiences, and even lying to medical practitioners back in Ireland about their abortion histories for fear of the censure such a revelation might provoke (Side 2011). These stories further highlighted the social inequalities around abortion travel that the

Eighth generated. While socio-economically privileged women with the means to travel for abortions regularly did so, those in more precarious socio-economic positions often faced far greater hardships in trying to do likewise (Side 2016). Some went so far as to place themselves in extremely vulnerable situations to fund an abortion journey, including obtaining loans from illegal moneylenders, or temporarily entering prostitution (Citizens Assembly 2017). Furthermore, in many of these cases this resulted in significantly later gestation terminations, which are more expensive, more invasive, and carry more risks of medical complications (Lentin 2013).

CONCLUSION

The authoritarian grip of control the church held over Irish peoples' sexual lives, but especially women's sexual lives, gradually loosened during the latter decades of the twentieth century (Daly 2016). What is surprising now is not the collapse of this sexual regime, but rather that it continued for so long. During the years of this extended church hegemony, sex was seen as sin, and anyone falling outside the strict normative sexual codes of behaviours set down by clerics were deemed sinners (Inglis 1998a). The social intolerance towards, in particular, unmarried mothers was acute. They represented a real and visible threat to the moral 'purity' that the newly independent Irish state imagined itself the virtuous upholder of (Fischer 2016). These idealised standards of sexual conduct were only ever a fantasy in reality. By the late 1960s, early 1970s, a younger generation of Irish women and Irish men were demanding a more liberal, less fundamentalist society, particularly around matters to do with sex, contraception, and women's role in society (Crowley 2013). When scandals involving clerical child sex abuse started to become public, much of the remaining authority the church had held over its congregation eroded even further. Through use of the courts, some liberalizations were achieved around access to contraception in the 1970s and 1980s, though reproductive freedom and abortion rights remained some distance off (Girvin 2018).

In 1981, the Pro-Life Amendment Campaign attempted to make Irish abortion laws even more restrictive by enshrining in the Constitution the right to life of the 'unborn' on an equal footing with the right to life of the mother. Critics at the time warned that due to the wording of the proposed amendment, this would inevitably result in risks to women's health, with doctors fearful they might incur prosecution if everything was not done to show equal regard for the life of the 'unborn' in cases involving difficult pregnancies. Nonetheless, in 1983 the amendment passed in a deeply divisive referendum, which one journalist memorably referred to as 'the second partitioning of Ireland' (Hesketh 1990). But as Earner-Byrne and Urquhart (2019) argue, what the Eighth amendment inadvertently achieved was to keep abortion politics permanently on the political radar in the Republic for the next three decades. A number of high-profile court cases relating to the Eighth Amendment's existence, public protests around abortion provision, as well as four more referenda on reproductive rights meant that the state's abortion drama was unfolding on a more or less constant basis. Throughout this time not only was Ireland's official pro-life stance looking increasingly isolated internationally. It was also looking more and more like a callous disregard for women's reproductive health. For, in reality, thousands of Irish women travelled abroad year on year for terminations of unwanted, unviable, or dangerous pregnancies, and Ireland's self-image as a proud pro-life nation could only be maintained by turning away from this reality.

In all this, it was only towards the latter years of the twentieth century that women's actual voices around their abortion histories began to be heard. With the church's 'moral monopoly' over sexuality persisting well into the 1970s, this ensured that abortion was rarely if ever discussed by women who had directly undergone the procedure. Thereafter, the passing of the Eighth Amendment all but guaranteed that silence, secrecy and shame came to dominate Irish women's abortion experiences. A 1988 Supreme Court ruling criminalising the provision of information on abortion services overseas further served to stigmatise women seeking abortions. This resulted in a pronounced culture of non-disclosure around women's abortion stories. By the turn of the century, however, such was the extent of the Irish abortion trail primarily to the United Kingdom that the traumatic realities of abortion in exile were commonplace knowledge in Irish society. At last, some women started to come forward with their testimonies of overseas terminations.

But another decade would pass—and, significantly, another major scandal implicating the Eighth Amendment would need to erupt in 2012—before personal abortion storytelling became a central feature of the Irish abortion debate. Only then would a culture of outspokenness by women about their abortions really take root. Only then would accounts like those from #twowomentravel enter mainstream public conversation on the realities of Ireland's abortion regime.

In the next chapter I turn my attention to this emerging phenomenon in recent years of Irish women speaking out publicly on their abortion histories.

REFERENCES

Arnold, B. (2009). *The Irish Gulag: How the state betrayed its innocent children*. Dublin: Gill & Macmillan.

Arveda Kissling, E. (2018). *From a whisper to a shout: Abortion activism and social media*. London: Repeater Books.

Bacik, I. (2004). *Kicking and screaming: Dragging Ireland into the twenty-first century*. Dublin: O'Brien Press.

Bacik, I. (2015). Abortion and the law in Ireland. In A. Quilty, S. Kennedy, & C. Conlon (Eds.), *The abortion papers Ireland: Volume 2* (pp. 104–117). Cork: Cork University Press.

Barry, U. (1988). Abortion in Ireland. *Feminist Review, 29*(2), 57–66.

BBC. (2016, August 22). *#TwoWomenTravel—Live-tweeting the journey for an abortion*. BBC. Available at https://www.bbc.com/news/blogs-trending-371 56673 (accessed 26 May 2020).

Beatty, A. (2013). Irish modernity and the politics of contraception, 1979–1993. *New Hibernia Review, 17*(3), 100–118.

Bloomer, F., & O'Dowd, K. (2014). Restricted access to abortion in the Republic of Ireland and Northern Ireland: Exploring abortion tourism and barrier to legal reform. *Culture, Health and Sexuality, 16*(4), 366–380.

Calkin, S. (2019). Healthcare not airfare! Art, abortion and political agency in Ireland. *Gender, Place & Culture, 26*(3), 338–361.

Canavan, J. (2012). Family and family change in Ireland: An overview. *Journal of Family Issues, 33*(2), 10–28.

Citizens' Assembly. (2017). *First report and recommendations of the Citizens' Assembly: The Eighth Amendment of the Constitution*. Dublin: Citizens' Assembly.

Connolly, L. (2002). *The Irish women's movement: From revolution to devolution*. New York: Palgrave.

Connor, D. (2018). Savita Halappanavar's parents call for Yes vote. *RTE*. Available at https://www.rte.ie/news/eighth-amendment/2018/0520/964749-savita-halappanavar/ (accessed 22 June 2018).

Constitution of Ireland. (1937). *Irish Constitution*. Dublin: Department of the Taoiseach.

Cox, C. (2009). Institutionalisation in Irish history and society. In M. McAuliffe, K. O'Donnell, & L. Lane (Eds.), *Palgrave advances in Irish history* (pp. 169–190). New York: Palgrave Macmillan.

Crowley, E. (2013). *Your place or mine? Community and belonging in 21st century Ireland.* Dublin: Orpen Press.

Crowley, U., & Kitchin, R. (2008). Producing "decent girls": Governmentality and the moral geographies of sexual conduct in Ireland. *Gender, Place and Culture: A Journal of Feminist Geography, 15*(4), 55–72.

Daly, M. (2006). Marriage, fertility and women's lives in twentieth-century Ireland (c.1900–c.1970). *Women's History Review, 15*(4), 571–585.

Daly, M. (2016). *Sixties Ireland: Reshaping the economy, state and society, 1957–1973.* Cambridge: Cambridge University Press.

de Londras, F., & Graham, L. (2013). Impossible floodgates and unworkable analogies in the Irish abortion debate. *Irish Journal of Legal Studies, 3*(3), 54–75.

Delay, C. (2018). Pills, potions, and purgatives: Women and abortion methods in Ireland, 1900–1950. *Women's History Review, 28*(3), 479–499.

de Londras, F., & Enright, M. (2018). *Repealing the 8th: Reforming Irish abortion law.* Bristol: Policy Press.

De Zordo, S., Mishtal, J., & Anton, L. (2016). *A fragmented landscape: Abortion governance and protest logics in Europe.* New York: Berghahn Books.

Dully, H. (2017). *Balance, binary debate and missing women: A discourse analysis and creative response to 30 years of the abortion debate on RTÉ current affairs television, 1983–2013.* Ph.D. dissertation, NUI Galway.

Earner-Byrne, L. (2007). *Mother and child: Maternity and child welfare in Dublin, 1922–1960.* Manchester: Manchester University Press.

Earner-Byrne, L., & Urquhart, D. (2019). *The Irish abortion journey, 1920–2018.* London: Palgrave.

Enright, M., & Cloatre, E. (2018). Transformative illegality: How condoms 'became legal' in Ireland, 1991–1993. *Feminist Legal Studies, 26*(3), 261–284.

Fahey, T., & Layte, R. (2007). Family and sexuality. In T. Fahey, H. Russell, & C. T. Whelan (Eds.), *Best of times? The social impact of the Celtic Tiger* (pp. 155–174). Dublin: Institute of Public Administration.

Farrell, E. (Ed.). (2012). *'She said she was in the family way': Pregnancy and infancy in modern Ireland.* London: The Institute of Historical Research.

Ferriter, D. (2009). *Occasions of sin: Sex and society in modern Ireland.* London: Profile Books.

Ferriter, D. (2014, August 23). The Irish abortion question has always been linked to class, secrecy and moral judgement. *Irish Times.* Available at https://www.irishtimes.com/news/social-affairs/the-irish-abortion-que

stion-has-always-been-linked-to-class-secrecy-and-moral-judgment-1.1905362 (accessed 26 May 2020).

Finnegan, F. (2004). *Do penance or perish: Magdalen Asylums in Ireland*. Oxford: Oxford University Press.

Fischer, C. (2016). Gender, nation, and the politics of shame: Magdalen laundries and the institutionalization of feminine transgression in modern Ireland. *Signs: Journal of Women in Culture and Society, 41*(4), 821–843.

Fischer, C. (2017). Revealing Ireland's "proper" heart: Apology, shame, nation. *Hypatia, 32*(4), 751–767.

Fischer, C. (2019). Abortion and reproduction in Ireland: Shame, nation-building and the affective politics of place. *Feminist Review, 122*(1), 32–48.

Fletcher, R. (1995). Silences: Irish women and abortion. *Feminist Review, 50*(1), 44–66.

Fletcher, R. (1998). "The pro-life" absolutes, feminist challenges: The fundamentalist narrative of Irish abortion law 1986–1992. *Osgoode Hall Law Journal, 36*(1), 1–62.

Fletcher, R. (2001). Post-colonial fragments: Representations of abortion in Irish law and politics. *Journal of Law and Society, 28*(4), 568–589.

Fletcher, R. (2018). #RepealingThe8th: Translating travesty, global conversation, and the Irish abortion referendum. *Feminist Legal Studies, 26*(3), 233–259.

Fogarty, M., Ryan, L., & Lee, J. (Eds.). (1984). *Irish values and attitudes: The Irish report of the European Value Systems Study*. Dublin: Dominican Publications.

Foley, D. (2019). "Too many children?": Family planning and *Humanae Vitae* in Dublin, 1960–1972. *Irish Economic and Social History, 46*(1), 142–160.

Fox, M., & Murphy, T. (1992). Irish abortion: Seeking refuge in a jurisprudence of doubt and delegation. *Journal of Law and Society, 19*(4), 454–466.

Francome, C. (1992). Irish women who seek abortions in England. *Family Planning Perspectives, 24*(6), 265–268.

Gilmartin, M., & White, A. (2011). Interrogating medical tourism: Ireland, abortion, and mobility rights. *Signs: Journal of Women in Culture and Society, 36*(2), 275–280.

Girvin, B. (2008). Contraception, moral panic and social change in Ireland, 1969–79. *Irish Political Studies, 23*(4), 555–576.

Girvin, B. (2018). An Irish solution to an Irish problem: Catholicism, contraception and change, 1922–1979. *Contemporary European History, 27*(1), 1–22.

Guttmacher Institute. (2016). *Fact sheet: Abortion in the United States*. Available at https://www.guttmacher.org/sites/default/files/factsheet/fb_induced_abortion_3.pdf (accessed 22 Nov 2019).

Harding, M. (2014). Irish abortion law: Legislating to stand still. *International Survey of Family Law, 20*(1), 201–226.

Healey, M. (2008). "I don't want to get into this, it's too controversial": How Irish women politicians conceptualise the abortion debate. In J. Schweppe (Ed.), *The unborn child, Article 40.3.3 and abortion in Ireland* (pp. 65–85). Dublin: Liffey Press.

Healy, G., Sheehan, B., & Whelan, N. (2015). *Ireland says yes: The inside story of how the vote for marriage equality was won.* Kildare: Merrion Press.

Hesketh, T. (1990). *The second partitioning of Ireland? The abortion referendum of 1983.* Dublin: Brandsma Books.

Hill, M. (2003). *Women in Ireland: A century of change.* Belfast: Blackstaff.

Hilliard, B. (2000). Motherhood, sexuality and the Catholic Church. In P. Kennedy (Ed.), *Motherhood in Ireland* (pp. 120–145). Cork: Mercier Press.

Hilliard, B. (2003). The Catholic Church and married women's sexuality: Habitus change in late 20th century Ireland. *Irish Journal of Sociology, 12*(2), 28–49.

Hogan, C. (2020). *Republic of Shame: Stories from Ireland's institutions for fallen women.* Dublin: Penguin Ireland.

Holland, K. (2013). *Savita: The tragedy that shook a nation.* Dublin: Transworld Ireland.

Holohan, C. (2018). *Reframing Irish youth in the sixties.* Liverpool: Liverpool University Press.

Hug, C. (1999). *The politics of sexual morality in Ireland.* Basingstoke: Palgrave Macmillan.

Inglis, T. (1997). Foucault, Bourdieu, and the field of Irish sexuality. *Irish Journal of Sociology, 6*(1), 5–28.

Inglis, T. (1998a). *Moral monopoly: The rise and fall of the Catholic Church in modern Ireland.* Dublin: University College Dublin.

Inglis, T. (1998b). *Lessons in Irish sexuality.* Dublin: University College Dublin Press.

Inglis, T. (1998c). From sexual repression to liberation? In M. Pellion & E. Slater (Eds.), *Encounters with modern Ireland* (pp. 121–142). Dublin: Institute of Public Administration.

Inglis, T. (2005). Origins and legacies of Irish prudery: Sexuality and social control in modern Ireland. *Éire-Ireland, 40*(2), 9–37.

Inglis, T. (2014). *Meanings of life in contemporary Ireland: Webs of significance.* London: Palgrave Macmillan.

Jackson, P. (1987). Outside the jurisdiction: Irishwomen seeking abortion. In C. Curtin, P. Jackson, & B. Connor (Eds.), *Gender in Irish society* (pp. 203–223). Galway: Galway University Press.

Kelly, F. (2018a, May 25). Yes vote shows overwhelming desire for change that nobody foresaw. *Irish Times.* Available at https://www.irishtimes.com/news/ireland/irish-news/yes-vote-shows-overwhelming-desire-for-change-that-nobody-foresaw-1.3508879 (accessed 25 May 2020).

Kelly, L. (2020). The contraceptive pill in Ireland *c*.1964–79: Activism, women and patient-doctor relationships. *Medical History, 64*(2), 195–218.

Kennedy, F. (2001). *Cottage to crèche: Family change in Ireland.* Dublin: The Institute of Public Administration.

Kitchin, R., & Lysaght, K. (2004). Sexual citizenship in Belfast, Northern Ireland. *Gender, Place & Culture, 11,* 83–103.

Kligman, G. (1998). *The politics of duplicity: Controlling reproduction in Ceausecu's Romania.* Berkeley: University of California Press.

Lentin, R. (2013). A woman died: Abortion and the politics of birth in Ireland. *Feminist Review, 105,* 130–136.

Luibheid, E. (2013). *Pregnant on arrival: Making the illegal immigrant.* St Paul: University of Minnesota Press.

Maguire, M. J. (2001). The changing face of Catholic Ireland: Conservatism and liberalism in the Ann Lovett and Kerry Babies scandals. *Feminist Studies, 27*(2), 335–358.

McAuliffe, M. (2009). Irish histories: Gender, women and sexualities. In M. McAuliffe, K. O'Donnell, & L. Lane (Eds.), *Palgrave advances in Irish history* (pp. 191–221). New York: Palgrave Macmillan.

McAvoy, S. (1999). The regulation of sexuality in the Irish Free State. In E. Malcom & G. Jones (Eds.), *Medicine, disease and the state in Ireland, 1650–1940* (pp. 253–266). Cork: Cork University Press.

McAvoy, S. (2004). Before Cadden: Abortion in mid-twentieth-century Ireland. In D. Keogh, F. O'Shea, & C. Quinlan (Eds.), *The lost decade: Ireland in the 1950s* (pp. 147–163). Cork: Cork University Press.

McAvoy, S. (2008). From anti-amendment campaigns to demanding reproductive justice: The changing landscape of abortion rights activism in Ireland, 1983–2008. In J. Schweppe (Ed.), *The unborn child, Article 40.3.3 and abortion in Ireland* (pp. 15–47). Dublin: Liffey Press.

McAvoy, S. (2012a). Its effect on public morality is vicious in the extreme: Defining birth control as obscene and unethical, 1926–32. In E. Farrell (Ed.), *She said she was in the family way: Pregnancy and infancy in modern Ireland* (pp. 35–52). London: Institute of Historical Research.

McAvoy, S. (2012b). A perpetual nightmare: Women, fertility control and the Irish state: The 1935 ban on contraceptives. In M. Preston & M. Ó hÓgartaigh (Eds.), *Gender and medicine in Ireland 1700–1950* (pp. 189–202). Syracuse: Syracuse University Press.

McCafferty, N. (1985). *A woman to blame: The Kerry Babies Case.* Dublin: Attic Press.

McCarthy, R. L. (2010). *Origins of the Magdalen laundries: An analytical history.* London: McFarland.

McGarry, P. (2018, July 28). How *Humanae Vitae* crushed the hopes of millions of Catholics. *Irish Times.* Available at https://www.irishtimes.com/

news/social-affairs/religion-and-beliefs/how-humanae-vitae-crushed-the-hopes-of-millions-of-catholics-1.3578547 (accessed 25 May 2020).

Muldowney, M. (2013). Breaking the silence on abortion: The 1983 referendum campaign. *History Ireland, 21*(2), 42–45.

Muldowney, M. (2015). Breaking the silence: Pro-choice activism in Ireland since 1983. In J. Redmond, S. Tiernan, S. McAvoy, & M. McAuliffe (Eds.), *Sexual politics in modern Ireland* (pp. 127–150). Dublin: Irish Academic Press.

Mullally, S. (2008). Abortion law: Rights discourse, dissent and reproductive autonomy. In J. Schweepe (Ed.), *The unborn child, Article 40.3.3 and abortion in Ireland: Twenty-five years of protection?* (pp. 213–245). Dublin: Liffey Press.

Mullally, U. (Ed.). (2018). *Repeal the 8th*. Dublin: Penguin.

Oaks, L. (2002). "Abortion is part of the Irish experience, it is part of what we are": The transformation of public discourse on Irish abortion policy. *Women's Studies International Forum, 25*(3), 315–333.

O'Carroll, S. (2012, February 6). Twenty years on: A timeline of the X case. *The Journal*. Available at https://www.thejournal.ie/twenty-years-on-a-timeline-of-the-x-case-347359-Feb2012/ (accessed 26 May 2020).

O'Connor, A. (1992). Abortion: Myths and realities from the Irish Folk Tradition. In A. Smyth (Ed.), *The Abortion Papers: Ireland* (pp. 57–65). Dublin: Attic Press.

O'Reilly, E. (1997). *Masterminds of the right*. Cork: Cork University Press.

O'Sullivan, E., & O'Donnell, I. (2012). *Coercive confinement in Ireland: Patients, prisoners and penitents*. Manchester: Manchester University Press.

O'Toole, F. (2003). The ugly politics of the womb. *Irish Times*. Available at https://www.irishtimes.com/opinion/the-ugly-politics-of-the-womb-1.368580 (accessed 25 May 2020).

Plummer, K. (2010). Generational sexualities, subterranean traditions, and the hauntings of the sexual world: Some preliminary remarks. *Symbolic Interaction, 33*(2), 163–190.

Porter, E. (1996). Culture, community and responsibilities: Abortion in Ireland. *Sociology, 30*(2), 279–298.

Quesney, A. (2015). Speaking up! Speaking out! Abortion in Ireland, exploring women's voices and contemporary abortion rights activism. In A. Quilty, S. Kennedy, & C. Conlon (Eds.), *The abortion papers Ireland: Volume 2* (pp. 150–164). Cork: Cork University Press, Cork.

Randall, V. (1992). Irish abortion politics: A comparative perspective. *The Canadian Journal of Irish Studies, 18*(2), 107–116.

Rattigan, C. (2008). "Crimes of passion of the worst character": Abortion cases and gender in Ireland, 1925–1950. In M. Gialanella Valiulis (Ed.), *Gender and power in Ireland* (pp. 115–140). Dublin: Irish Academic Press.

Rattigan, C. (2012). *What else could I do? Single mothers and infanticide, Ireland 1900–1950*. Dublin: Irish Academic Press.

Rose, R. S. (1978). Induced abortion in the Republic of Ireland. *British Journal of Criminology, 18*(3), 253–254.

Rossiter, A. (2009). *Ireland's hidden diaspora: The abortion trail and the making of a London-Irish underground*. London: IASC Publishing.

Ruane, M. (2000). *The Irish journey: Women's stories of abortion*. Dublin: Irish Family Planning Association.

Ryan, L. (2007). "A decent girl well worth helping": Women, migration and unwanted pregnancy. In L. Harte & Y. Whelan (Eds.), *Ireland beyond boundaries: Mapping Irish studies in the twenty-first century* (pp. 135–153). Dublin: Pluto Press.

Sanger, C. (2017). *About abortion: Terminating pregnancy in 21-st century America*. New York: Harvard University Press.

Schweppe, J. (2008). Introduction. In J. Schweppe (Ed.), *The unborn child, Article 40.3.3 and abortion in Ireland* (pp. 1–14). Dublin: Liffey Press.

Sheldon, S. (2018). Empowerment and privacy? Home use of abortion pills in the Republic of Ireland. *Signs, 43*(4), 823–849.

Side, K. (2011). A B and C. versus Ireland: A new beginning to access legal abortion in the Republic of Ireland? *International Feminist Journal of Politics, 13*(3), 390–412.

Side, K. (2016). A geopolitics of migrant women, mobility and abortion access in the Republic of Ireland. *Gender, Place & Culture, 23*(12), 1788–1799.

Siggins, L. (2016, April 11). RTE told us our abortion film lacked balance. *Irish Times*. Available at https://www.irishtimes.com/life-and-style/people/rt%C3%A9-told-us-our-abortion-film-lacked-balance-1.2602308 (accessed 26 May 2020).

Smyth, A. (1995). States of change: Reflections on Ireland in several uncertain parts. *Feminist Review, 50*, 24–43.

Smyth, L. (1998). Narratives of Irishness and the problem of abortion: The X Case 1992. *Feminist Review, 60*, 61–83.

Smyth, L. (2005). *Abortion and nation*. New York: Routledge.

Smyth, L. (2015). Ireland's abortion ban: Honour, shame, and the possibility of a moral revolution. In A. Quilty, S. Kennedy, & C. Conlon (Eds.), *The abortion papers Ireland: Volume 2* (pp. 167–178). Cork: Cork University Press.

Solinger, R. (2005). *Pregnancy and power: A short history of reproductive politics in America*. New York: NYU Press.

Solomons, M. (1992). *Pro life? The Irish question*. Dublin: Lilliput Press.

Speed, A. (1992). The struggle for reproductive rights: A brief history in its political context. In A. Smyth (Ed.), *The abortion papers* (pp. 85–98). Dublin: Attic Press.

Stopper, A. (2005). *Mondays at Gaj's: The story of the Irish Women's Liberation Movement*. Dublin: Liffey Press.

Two Women Travel. (2016a, August 20). *boarding, it's chilly. @endakennyTD.* Twitter. Available at https://twitter.com/twowomentravel?lang=en (accessed 25 May 2020).

Two Women Travel. (2016b, August 20). *We stand in solidarity with all women exiled @EndaKennyTD, his predecessors, his apologists.* Twitter. Available at https://twitter.com/twowomentravel?lang=en (accessed 25 May 2020).

Two Women Travel. (2016c, August 20). *pretty ordinary sights, in a place away from home, can't say it's comforting, though @endakennyTD.* Twitter. Available at https://twitter.com/twowomentravel?lang=en (accessed 25 May 2020).

Two Women Travel. (2016d, August 21). *@endakennyTD forced by more Irish in waiting room.* Twitter. Available at https://twitter.com/twowomentravel?lang=en (accessed 25 May 2020).

Two Women Travel. (2016e, August 21). *@endakennytd all done and dusted, we won't get home for another 24hrs.* Twitter. Available at https://twitter.com/twowomentravel?lang=en (accessed 25 May 2020).

Two Women Travel. (2016f, August 21). *Not for the first or the last time a bleeding woman about to face a long treck home.* Twitter. Available at https://twitter.com/twowomentravel?lang=en (accessed 25 May 2020).

Two Women Travel. (2016g, August 21). *We are nearly home. Thanks to everyone for unreal support—with one glaring exception. @endakennyTD.* Twitter. Available at https://twitter.com/twowomentravel?lang=en (accessed 25 May 2020).

Two Women Travel. (2016h, August 21). *A series of waiting rooms, a sequence of tediums.* Twitter. Available at https://twitter.com/twowomentravel?lang=en (accessed 25 May 2020).

Wanrooij, B. P. F. (1999). Italy: Sexuality, morality and public authority. In F. X. Eder, L. A. Hall, & G. Hekma (Eds.), *Sexual cultures in Europe: National histories* (pp. 114–138). Manchester: Manchester University Press.

Waterson, J., & Duncan, P. (2018). Irish anti-abortion campaigners dodge Google's ad ban. *Guardian.* Available at https://www.theguardian.com/world/2018/may/24/irish-anti-abortion-campaigners-dodge-google-ad-ban (accessed 28 May 2020).

CHAPTER 3

First-Person Abortion Story-Sharing as Key Pro-choice Strategy

Abstract This chapter argues that first-person abortion story-sharing was a key tactic of pro-choice groups supporting the removal of the Eighth Amendment from the Constitution. This chapter shows that what these groups achieved was a remarkable normalising of abortion talk by supporting women who had undergone abortion to speak publicly about their experiences. In this, these women storytellers were mirroring certain pro-choice movements in other contexts, where a new 'sound it loud, say it proud' narrative around abortion experiences has emerged in recent years as a central strategy for destigmatising abortion discourse. Post-abortion, in most countries the norm remains self-censorship of their history of terminating an unwanted pregnancy. In the Irish situation, this silencing has been pronounced, with women's experiences long excluded from public debates on abortion. However, in the years preceding and throughout the campaign to repeal the Eighth, something changed. And what changed was that women found their voice.

Keywords Abortion story-sharing · Repeal · Savita Halappanavar · Abortion stigma

© The Author(s) 2020   39
D. Ralph, *Abortion and Ireland*,
https://doi.org/10.1007/978-3-030-58692-8_3

INTRODUCTION

The main civil society grouping that fought throughout the 2018 Repeal referendum to have Ireland's abortion legislation amended was called Together For Yes. In April 2019 *Time* magazine named Together For Yes's three co-directors Ailbhe Smyth, Grainne Griffin and Orla O'Connor on its list of 'world's 100 most influential people' for their work on the 2018 campaign that dramatically repudiated the Eighth Amendment (Armstrong 2019). This was a major accolade for the three co-directors, and was warmly welcomed by Repeal supporters in Ireland. At the same time, this international recognition was also heartening to pro-choice groups beyond Irish shores where abortion restrictions remain onerous, or where women's reproductive rights are currently under threat (RTE 2019). In these jurisdictions, abortion advocates are hoping the momentum generated by the Repeal victory will inspire their struggles to counter resurgent anti-abortion groups in their home countries. In this respect, 2018 will in all likelihood be remembered as the most momentous year in the Irish abortion landscape.

Yet a case could be made that 2012 was equally crucial, if not perhaps more so. Having languished on the political fringes for a considerable time, this was the year that the vexed question over what to do about Ireland's strict and—as it would transpire—at times fatally dangerous abortion ban moved decisively back centre stage (Murray 2016). For one thing, 2012 marked the twentieth anniversary of the notorious 1992 X Case. And to coincide with this, several pro-choice advocacy groups across the country had set about organising public events, speak-outs and publication launches, as well as making numerous submissions to elected representatives for legislative action on the matter (O'Carroll 2012). As part of these commemorations, in February the National Women's Council of Ireland held a major public meeting titled 'From X to ABC: 20 Years of Inaction on Reproductive Rights' to highlighting the ongoing legal vacuum surrounding abortion access (National Women's Council of Ireland 2012).

Meanwhile, in April, *Irish Times* journalist Kathy Sheridan published a story that in the Irish context was, simply, extraordinary. In it, Sheridan interviewed four women who had undergone terminations abroad, detailing their ordeals of being forced to travel and the associated financial and health costs they endured (Sheridan 2018). But what was remarkable here was that, as well as their photographs, the women had agreed to have their full names used in the article. Their names were Amanda Mellet, Ruth Bowie, Arlette Lyons and Jenny McDonald (Sheridan 2018). The pioneering story was published on the front page of the newspaper, and the response was a swell of public sympathy for the quartet. That same month a bill was brought before the parliament by Deputy Claire Daly attempting to give effect to the X Case ruling (Griffin et al. 2019). The bill was defeated in the chamber by 101 votes to 27, but again it gave the issue of Ireland's unresolved abortion question the oxygen of publicity (Griffin et al. 2019). Then in July the Abortion Rights Campaign was founded, a pro-choice lobby group that organised the first March For Choice in Dublin that September (Abortion Rights Campaign 2016).

Also in July of 2012 a Dublin-wide advertising campaign by the anti-abortion group Youth Defence was launched, this time pushing the abortion issue into the public arena in a highly contentious fashion (Hyland 2012). The campaign saw billboards hung outside all the major train, bus and light-rail stations, and contained an image of a forlorn-looking young woman's face that had been ripped down the centre, alongside the caption, 'Abortion Tears Her Life Apart' (Thompson 2018). This expensive and controversial campaign, however, seemed to backfire on the pro-life lobby group. When canvassed for their views by the media, many members of the travelling public found the billboards offensive and overly aggressive, while later hundreds of complaints were lodged with the Advertising Standards Authority (Kennedy 2013).

But it was an incident that occurred in an Irish hospital in October of 2012 that would irreversibly alter the course of Irish abortion history. The incident in question, which will be discussed in detail later in this chapter, involved the shocking death of a pregnant woman named Savita Halappanavar who entered a maternity ward complaining of abdominal pains. Ms. Halappanavar happened to miscarry her pregnancy (Holland 2013). But as a foetal heartbeat could be detected throughout the miscarriage, she was repeatedly denied a termination. Due to a lack of intervention by hospital staff her blood became infected; she died of septic shock a week after arriving seeking medical help. When details of Ms. Halappanavar's fate became public, the story became a news sensation not only in Ireland but across the world, shining once more a harsh spotlight on the country's abortion laws. The *Indian Times* ran with the headline, 'Ireland Murders Pregnant Indian Dentist' (cited in O'Carroll 2018). Later, her husband Praveen Halappanavar was reported at the inquest in his wife's death as describing her treatment at the hands of the Irish health system as 'barbaric, horrendous, inhuman' (cited in Cullen 2013, para. 1).

The argument I present in this chapter is that the tragic death of Savita Halappanavar in 2012 proved a game-changer in the seemingly endless struggle for abortion rights in Ireland. Successive rounds of polling data showed that support to change Ireland's abortion laws had been gaining momentum for some time (McCarthy 2018). However, in the months and years following Ms. Halappanavar's death, this support was galvanised. Public outrage was palpable at the needless, tragic demise of this young woman, and various pro-choice groups demonstrated loudly in towns and cities across the country for immediate change to Ireland's draconian abortion laws (Holland 2013). At the same time—and what was unique here, I argue—was that women who had long remained silent about their abortion histories now began to publicly share their experiences across a range of public fora in an attempt to influence the national dialogue on abortion. What De Zordo et al. (2016) term the 'protest logics' of pro-choice advocates shifted, with women's voices now centre stage in that logic. In the sections that follow, I outline how many pro-choice women became, in a manner of speaking, 'pro-voice', challenging the habitual muting or side-lining of their abortion experiences. In so doing, and in becoming abortion storytellers, they helped to contribute to the normalising of abortion talk in the Republic of Ireland. And this normalisation not only showed how common abortion was in Irish life but was also a key factor in influencing the vote in May 2018 to overturn the Eighth Amendment.

In making this argument I analyse a range of political figures' public statements around the Repeal referendum, the print and broadcast media's portrayal of the campaign, as well as pro-choice advocacy organisations' publicity materials on Repeal. In addition, I analyse various online sites such as Twitter, The X-ile Project and, in particular, *In Her Shoes*, a Facebook page dedicated exclusively to women sharing stories of their abortion histories. Conceptually, the chapter draws on the extensive literature utilising a contact theory approach (Cockrill and Biggs 2018; Cowan 2014) and a social movement theory approach (Cockrill 2014; Kimport 2012; Ludlow 2012; Polletta 2006) showing how the act of publicly sharing abortion stories can help 'normalise' a procedure that has long been stigmatised and discredited in society. In brief, contact theory is a theory on how intergroup conflict between two opposing groups can be potentially reduced and even eliminated by meaningful contact between members of opposing social groups. Social movement theory is a theory explaining how in certain circumstances social actors can mobilise collectively to successfully advance claims for social change.

Before elaborating on each of these theories, however, I detail how the Eighth Amendment contributed directly to Savita Halappanavar's demise.

IRELAND, THE EIGHTH AND SAVITA

In September 1983, as detailed in the previous chapter, the Irish voted to insert Article 40.3.3 into the Constitution, a forty-three word amendment that placed the right to life of a pregnant woman on a legal par with that of her 'unborn' child. Known as the Eighth Amendment, the referendum passed by majority, and made the legislation dating back to the 1861 Offenses Against the Person Act that criminalised abortion even more restrictive than it had been for the past century and a half (O'Connor 1992).

In the thirty-five years of the Eight Amendment's existence, those forty-three words brutalised countless Irish women and girls who found themselves carrying unwanted, unplanned, or wanted but unviable pregnancies (Mullally 2018). Until recent years, the X Case received the most stinging criticism by opponents of the Amendment, involving as it did a fourteen-year-old girl who was pregnant as a result of rape and whom the state was attempting to prevent from travelling abroad for an abortion. At the time demonstrators took to the streets in support of the girl, marching behind banners reading, 'Licence To Rape', 'Scrape The Eighth', 'Internment Nation' (cited in Earner-Byrne and Urquhart 2019, 86). However, eighteen years later, the X Case was still making headlines. In 2010 the Grand Chamber of the European Court of Human Rights ruled in favour of three women who brought the Irish state to the European courts for the Eighth Amendment's failure to clarify when precisely a lawful abortion is permissible in Ireland (Murray 2016). The applicants, known only as Miss A, Miss B and Miss C, argued that the criminalisation of abortion in Ireland and its widespread inaccessibility had endangered their rights to health, well-being and life during their pregnancies, and as such was a breach of the European Convention of Human Rights (Staunton 2011). Applicant C's case was seen as particularly callous, as the woman was in remission from aggressive cancer when she became pregnant but was refused a termination by the Ethics Committee of a maternity hospital because her life was not at 'immediate risk' as a result of the pregnancy.

The 17 judges in the Chamber ruled unanimously in favour of Misses A, B and C, decreeing that in the absence of legalisation on abortion provision following the X Case ruling, all three applicants had been subject to cruel, inhuman and degrading treatment at the hands of the state. The Court ruled that the government must legislate for abortion immediately (Staunton 2011).

The government did not. Instead, the government dragged its heels on implementing the Grand Chamber's ruling that the Irish state provide clarity on when precisely legal abortions were available to protect the mother's life (O'Carroll 2012). And in the meantime, as it procrastinated once more, arguably the Eighth's most flagrant failure to protect even the basic human rights of pregnant women occurred in an Irish hospital in 2012. On 21 October that year, Savita Halappanavar presented at a maternity ward in Galway in the West of Ireland (Holland 2013). She was seventeen weeks pregnant, and was complaining of back pain. Discharged without a diagnosis, later that day she returned to the hospital with severe vaginal pain. It emerged this time that she was miscarrying her foetus. A week later, Ms. Halappanavar left that same hospital dead from septic shock after being repeatedly denied an abortion because a foetal heartbeat could be detected throughout her miscarriage (Holland 2013). Official hospital records showed that Ms. Halappanavar had requested a termination as soon as it was clear she was miscarrying (Health Services Executive 2013). The records further noted that the doctors' 'assessment of the legal context in which their clinical professional judgement was to be exercised' meant they had to 'await events'—that is, they had to wait for the foetus to expire before they could intervene (Health Services Executive 2013, 5). The Halappanavars repeatedly requested a termination, but each time were refused. The inquest into her death heard how the midwife manager turned down one such request by explaining to Ms. Halappanavar and her husband Praveen, 'This is a Catholic country' (cited in RTE 2013, para. 1). On 23 October Ms. Halappanavar delivered her foetus spontaneously, then she went into a coma. Transferred to intensive care on 28 October as her medical team attempted to treat her for septicaemia arising as a result of her prolonged miscarriage, Ms. Halappanavar went into cardiac arrest and died at 1.09 a.m. (Holland 2013).

Kitty Holland, the journalist who broke the Savita Halappanavar story on 17 November, said that there has been 'myriad crises' arising as a direct consequence of the 1983 referendum result that all made shocking headlines (Holland 2013). But from the outset, the crisis involving Savita

Halappanavar was different. And primarily what was different was that—unlike A, B, C, X and a number of other cases—this time the life of the woman at the centre of the tragedy was not hidden behind a letter of the alphabet or any other euphemism. This time the woman was straight away *named* in the media. In the immediate aftermath of her doomed pregnancy, Praveen Halappanavar told reporters from all the country's main media outlets of his and his wife Savita's ordeal once they arrived at Galway maternity hospital (O'Carroll 2018). He described at length the series of events that led up to Ms. Halappanavar's death, and these, along with several photos of her smiling enthusiastically with a bindi on her forehead and seemingly healthy and happy, were broadcast widely on television, in newspapers, across a range of social media platforms.

Originally from India, Savita Halappanavar lived in Galway with her husband Praveen. She was a trainee dentist there, having moved to the West of Ireland to complete her studies (Holland 2013). She was one of the main organisers of a popular Indian-Irish annual festival in Galway, and by all accounts she was well-liked in the community. She had a friendly, open manner. She was full of energy. She was incredibly excited about becoming a mother. She was a young woman in the prime of life. She was just 31 years old when she presented with signs of an impending miscarriage to hospital staff in Galway. Expert gynaecological testimony into her death concluded that her life had been cut short because of the existence of the Eighth Amendment (Health Services Executive 2013).

In the public and media debates that followed, Savita Halappanavar soon became known simply and affectionately as 'Savita' (Whelan 2012). In the years since, her name has become a household one in any debate on Ireland's abortion regime. Her story, and the details that emerged of her scandalous fate at the hands of the Irish health care system, was one other people could identify with, especially other young women. And this was pointedly so because of the very public nature of her demise. 'Savita' wasn't just another letter in the alphabet. People felt they knew 'Savita'. Commentators agreed that the rolling coverage of her death had acted as a 'catalyst' in igniting a latent pro-choice movement, in particular among a generation of younger activists without direct memories of the X Case and other Eighth-related controversies (Mullally 2018).

The political temperature surrounding Ireland's abortion legalisation soared, and public outrage was palpable as news spread of how it was the Eighth Amendment that had prevented Ms. Halappanavar from receiving a termination when she requested one (Holland 2013). Numerous pro-choice activist groups mobilised in the wake her death, and momentum to bring change to the three-decades-long political impasse over abortion in Ireland gathered pace. Within days of the story becoming public, an incensed crowd of upwards of 20,000 marched throughout the streets of Dublin and chanted, 'NEVER AGAIN, NEVER AGAIN, NEVER AGAIN' (RTE 2012). In the weeks following, sit-ins and candle-lit vigils were organised, while further large-scale street demonstrations demanding a change to the country's abortion legislation were held in Dublin, Galway, Cork, as well as outside the Irish embassies in London, Berlin and Brussels (RTE 2012). The midwife's remark about Ireland being a Catholic country was picked up by the international media. This was shaming for the government, and reputational damage followed with reputed global figures calling the country's laws not only out of step with the rest of the modern world but also medieval and misogynistic (Specia 2018). Indeed, an analysis of media framings of 'the Savita story' in the year after her passing showed how one of the main 'storylines' to develop out of the event was how public opinion had been galvanised into shifting firmly to a 'middle ground' position whereby the status quo on abortion had now become intolerable, and legislative change was imperative (McDonnell and Murphy 2019).

In 2014 the government was further embarrassed over its inaction on the X Case ruling. In this instance, the case involved that of a clinically dead woman who was fifteen weeks pregnant when she died suddenly in hospital (McDonald 2014). Medics and lawyers for the hospital clutched at the Constitution unsure if they would be subject to criminal prosecution for turning off the woman's life support machine while her foetus remained alive in utero. Only three weeks later, after the case had been through the High Court, was the state satisfied it had fully vindicated the right to life of the 'unborn', having heard expert medical testimony that the now eighteen week-old foetus would have no chance of survival outside the womb of its already dead mother (Butler 2016). By this stage the nameless woman's internal organs had begun to rot and her head become disfigured as her swelling brain put pressure on her cranium. For the entire three weeks since her untimely death, her family had begged the authorities to end their ordeal and let them bury the woman 'with dignity' (Carolan 2019).

Almost six years on from Ms. Halappanavar's death, jubilant scenes erupted at the announcement of the official vote tally outside Dublin

Castle on 26 May 2018. The myth that Ireland was an abortion-free holdout against the tide of sexual permissiveness and moral laxity sweeping the rest of the modern world was finally over. The result was described variously in the media as a stunning victory, an emphatic win, a landslide success and a Big Yes (O'Brien and Armstrong 2018). Other commentators likened the scale of the Repeal victory to a 'reproductive rebellion' that ended once and for all the offshoring of Ireland's abortion problem (Kasstan and Crook 2018). And the Amendment responsible for a litany of grotesque and frightening situations that women endured in private in bedrooms and bathrooms across the country, and at times much more publicly in hospital wards and courthouses, was no more.

Ireland was in the international media spotlight again over its abortion legislation, but this time for very different reasons. In an almost perfect reversal of the 1983 result, 66.4 per cent of voters agreed to repeal the Eighth (Connor 2018). Hearing the result, an outpouring of relief that the referendum had passed spread through the crowd packed into the courtyard of Dublin Castle. Many were in tears, many dancing with joy. A chant started up, ringing round the courtyard's walls as it was repeated over and over for the next several minutes (McCarthy 2018).

Tellingly, the crowd chanted, 'SAVITA, SAVITA, SAVITA.'

ACHIEVING A 'REPRODUCTIVE REBELLION': THEORETICAL UNDERPINNINGS

So, it is worth asking, how was this 'reproductive rebellion' achieved? This 'Big Yes'? I argue in the remainder of this chapter that a central mechanism in leveraging a latent pro-choice sentiment among people was to foreground the abortion testimonies of women. In this section I consider two theoretical frameworks—contact theory and social movement theory—to try to understand how sharing abortion stories can help quell the discrediting connotations attaching to this particular medical intervention. Taken together, these paired conceptual lens support the contention that by talking about abortion—openly, freely, genuinely—the stigma surrounding it will be reduced, the procedure normalised. Proponents of both contact theory and social movement theory show how stories resonate in the public consciousness, particularly stories that contradict the status quo and dominant social narratives surrounding abortion. In effect, both theoretical traditions offer evidence that promoting abortion talk is an effective tactic in promoting greater public empathy for women's reproductive rights around pregnancy terminations. I first consider contact theory, then social movement theory.

Gordon Allport's (1954) 'contact theory' states that appropriate contact between two groups can help mitigate and decrease intergroup prejudice. Originally devised in the 1950s to test whether meaningful reductions in racial bias could be achieved between majority whites and minority blacks in the segregationist United States, Allport found that, under certain conditions, social contact between the two groups produced a lessening of race-based prejudice. Analogously, sociologists working in the Allport tradition of contact theory have found that intransigence in attitudes towards abortion has been demonstrated to alter when abortion secrets are disclosed. Cockrill and Biggs (2018), in an experiment involving a book club intervention, paired together pro-choice and pro-life women where they discussed over several weeks a collection of non-fiction stories that included incidents of pregnancy terminations. The results were that, after discussing the material in the book club as equals, and where at least one woman made a disclosure of her abortion history, demonstrable changes in attitudes towards women's reproductive decisions emerged. Cockrill and Biggs's (2018, 345) findings suggested that 'exposure to the stories of women who have had abortions can reduce abortion stigma'.

Similarly, Cowan (2014, 2017) found that while orientations to abortion are often embedded in individuals' world views, those world views themselves are amenable to change. Her research discovered that those who had listened to disclosures of abortion end up having, as she states, 'a more accurate understanding of how common abortion is, who has them and why' (Cowan 2014, 465). On the other hand, those who had not been exposed to disclosures of abortion secrets believed they did not know any women who had had an abortion, and this influenced their views that abortion access should be severely curtailed, or even outright illegal.

Social movement theory offers a second and complementary sociological lens through which to understand how abortion stigma may be quelled through abortion story-sharing. Social movement theorists are clear that narrative and storytelling are central to any movement's organisational identity (Polletta et al. 2011). The stories a movement tells serve to frame the movement itself and to foster group cohesion. Francesca Polletta (2002, 48) states that, as for why movement members tell stories, 'they probably do so to sustain and strengthen members' commitment'.

Fine (1995, 132) argues that movement stories are a bundle of narratives—composed of 'war stories', 'horror stories', and 'happy-ending stories'—each of which 'plays upon the emotions of participants' and strengthens commitment to shared goals. Yet movement stories do not solely play upon the emotions of already existing members. They have an influence beyond internally structuring and organising the in-group, or what Martin (2015) calls a 'spillover effect'. That is, movement stories also arouse the emotions of those outside the group, working in many cases to persuade non-members to become sympathetic to the movement's aims, as well as recruiting new members to the movement. At the same time, movement stories in most instances are better viewed as 'counter-narratives' rather than simply 'narratives'. Since most social movements generally operate in an antagonistic relationship with dominant social structures, their express purpose is to challenge and change pre-existing systems of power, hierarchy and domination. As such, the stories most social movements tend to tell are alternative stories to dominant social narratives, or, in a word, counter-narratives (Martin 2015).

Like many other social movements, pro-choice movements in many parts of the world have recognised the value of abortion story-sharing to their movement aspirations. To this end, many have carefully crafted abortion narratives with the aim of evoking greater public support for access to safe, legal and free abortion services. In most such movements, there is a foregrounding of what Ludlow (2008) terms 'politically necessary' and 'politically acceptable' abortion stories. The former include cases where women seek abortions as a result of rape, incest and emotionally/physically abusive partners. The latter includes cases where women seek abortions as a result of contraceptive failure, crisis pregnancies, and fatal foetal anomalies. In a variety of contexts, such stories of necessity and acceptability have been labelled the 'hard cases', or, following Fine's (1995) definition, 'horror stories'. They represent formula stories that have been routinely deployed to bolster support for abortion rights and legislative change (Martin et al. 2017). However, it is recognised that there has been a narrative rigidity around abortion story-sharing among pro-choice advocates, and that a third category of abortion story rarely if ever gets articulated in pro-choice rhetoric and discursive repertoires. Ludlow (2008) calls such abortion stories 'the things we cannot say', and include the accounts of women who have had multiple abortions, those who have experienced regret and grief post-abortion, and those who seek abortions simply because they do not want to be pregnant at a particular time, or so-called 'elective' or 'convenience' abortions. Scholar here have acknowledged that such stories may make sympathetic narratives difficult to craft and that, in the main, these narratives have been absent in pro-choice discourse (Allen 2014; Ludlow 2012; Martin et al. 2017; Baird and Millar 2019).

That said, a renewed focus of a new generation of pro-choice abortion campaigners in many parts of the world has been to encourage all forms of personal storytelling by women of their abortion experiences (Kimport 2012). Here, women from all over the globe have contributed first-hand abortion accounts to an evolving conversation on what abortion is 'really' like. There is a greater flexibility in these narratives, with storytellers going well beyond the 'hard cases' and 'horror stories' to include accounts of what may be deemed 'routine abortions' and positive accounts of the procedure not inflected by shame, regret, sadness (Cockrill 2014; Kumar 2013). These are a relatively new form of abortion story, or to paraphrase Ludlow, such accounts are becoming 'the things we *can* say'. One study has coined the phrase 'happy abortions' to account for this little-discussed pregnancy termination experience (Millar 2017).

Both contact theory and social movement theory should be seen as complementing one another here in this effort to better understand how abortion talk can contribute to the normalisation and destigmatisation of the procedure. The focus of contact theory remains intra-group face-to-face contact to reduce overall prejudice between in- and out-group members, while social movement stories can be disseminated among both in-group members as well as via as a variety of public fora to raise movement awareness and recruit new members. Taken together, contact theory and social movement theory offer a way of framing how, in certain contexts and under certain situations, greater public sympathy for women's access to abortion services can emerge. The more people hear about abortion, and from the voices of women who have actually had them, it is anticipated the more compassion people will ultimately have for women who seek abortions. If non-disclosure of abortion experiences remains the cultural norm, then the discrediting stigma attaching to women who undergo the procedure will continue.

There is no doubt that in recent decades subjects long deemed undiscussable in many Western countries have been gradually uncloseted, opened up to public debate and scrutiny like never before. Depression, divorce, domestic violence, homosexuality, miscarriage, infertility,

HIV/AIDS and cancer—all topics once considered taboo—are no longer obscured in veils of silence or euphemism (Andeweg 2017; Escoffier 2003). Rather, such matters are routinely the focus of lively debate by politicians, pundits, journalists and celebrities, as they are too by ordinary individuals having what are by now ordinary conversations around once-difficult-to-broach matters. Through such public debate—alongside public protest and legal reform in some instances—these concerns have moved from a discursive realm dominated largely by shame, stigma and silence to one where frank, candid and open discussion is possible (Herzog 2011).

In short, though still subject to controversy, dispute and contestation, debating such issues has become normalised. In next section I detail how an unprecedented culture of abortion disclosure emerged in recent years in the Republic of Ireland in an effort to persuade a critical mass into supporting the repeal of the legalisation that had banned abortion access in the country.

Repeal, Pro-choice Activism and Storytelling

In all, 1,429,981 people voted to repeal the Eighth as opposed to 732,632 who voted to retain it (RTE 2018). With the second highest voter turnout ever for a referendum issue at 64.13 per cent of the electorate, this was a resounding two-to-one victory for the Repeal side. And in its effort to convince the electorate that the Eighth be removed from the Constitution, the Repeal movement drew on all the familiar campaigning strategies of door-to-door canvassing, distributing pro-choice merchandise and information leaflets, erecting campaign posters on lampposts and other public spaces (Griffin et al. 2019). Their spokespersons appeared on numerous current affairs programmes on television and radio debating the demerits of the current regime with abortion opponents. Demonstrations were organised across the country. Since it was first held in 2013, thousands of pro-choice activists, lawyers, doctors, midwives and ordinary citizens took to the streets of Dublin every year in the annual March For Choice (de Londras and Enright 2018). Their numbers swelling year on year, they marched under traditional pro-choice banners and placards like 'Get Your Rosaries Off My Ovaries', 'My Body, My Choice', 'Not The Church, Not The State, Women Must Decide Their Fate' (cited in Mullally 2018). People wearing pro-choice badges, stickers, tee-shirts and the visually striking black jumpers with a white-embossed REPEAL logo in san-serif script were distinctly visible in many parts of the country well in advance of the vote.

But when exit pollsters asked what were the 'referendum influencing factors', it is significant that a mere 10 per cent of voters cited 'campaign posters' as influencing how their vote was decided, and only a further 7 per cent cited 'direct contact with campaigners' (McShane 2018). Instead, 37 per cent of those polled cited 'the experiences of people I know', while a further 43 per cent cited 'peoples' personal stories as covered in the media' (McShane 2018). This strongly suggested that traditional political canvassing tactics had far less clout in determining how the vote was swayed on the Eighth. And what struck a chord in this refer- endum with a staggering 80 per cent of voters was the abortion narratives that women had shared face to face with people or that people had learned of in the media. My argument in what follows here is that Savita Halappanavar's death was a game-changer regarding abortion storytelling in contemporary Ireland.

Since she died in 2012 the culture of abortion disclosure in Ireland has changed, with 'the abortion debate' now very much centred on women as the key experts to any understanding of the issue. For instance, following Ms. Halappanavar's very public demise, a number of prominent public figures came out in support of Repeal and in the process told of their own abortion experiences for the first time. One of the first in this mould was Roisin Ingle, columnist and host of the popular 'Roisin Meets Podcast', who in September 2015 wrote in the *Irish Times* of her own abortion fifteen years previously (Ingle 2015). Her account in the Saturday edition of the paper sparked widespread discussion of abortion on television, on radio and online all that weekend, with Ingle herself being interviewed by all the main broadcasters in the days following the publication of her abortion story. Ingle's (2015, para. 3) account was more in the mould of the 'routine abortion' narrative, with the journalist stating of her experi- ence, 'This is not a sad story.' She did, however, cite the Savita case as a catalyst behind her 'coming out' narrative.

The following week, well-known Irish actor and comedian Tara Flynn spoke of her non-traumatic abortion experience in the Netherlands in 2006 on a stage at the Electric Picnic festival, the biggest outdoor music festival in Ireland (Flynn 2015). Flynn's disclosure in a packed tent in front of a live audience was widely reported in all the Irish media in the days following, and like Ingle's, Flynn's account was neither a 'hard case' nor a 'horror story'. Meantime, in October 2015, Helen Lenihen appeared alongside her well-known writer/director husband Graham Lenihen in an Amnesty International promotional video calling on the Irish government to decriminalise abortion (Gentleman 2015). In the video, Mrs. and Mr. Lenihen spoke of Helen's abortion in London in 2004 when she discovered she was carrying an unviable pregnancy. The Lenihens' story was picked up by numerous media outlets both nationally and internationally.

Running alongside these public figures going on the record with their abortion experiences were any number of private women who had no immediate public platform but who also wanted to disclose the details of their abortions. The *Irish Times* ran scores of stories of women who had had abortions in the months following the Savita Hallapanavar case, and in a section titled 'Abortion and Me' the paper invited readers in the weeks before the referendum to submit their abortion stories for publication (*Irish Times* 2018b). While some of the contributors here claimed they deeply regretted their abortion decision, a significant majority wrote that abortion was the best decision for them at the time. Similar contributions on abortion were published in the *Irish Independent*, *Irish Examiner*, *Sunday Independent*, and the *Sunday Business Post*. Further to this, numerous television and radio programmes all featured women speaking publicly and plainly about their abortion experiences.

Arguably the most audacious of all these acts of public abortion story-sharing came, as described at the outset of Chapter 2, from an Irish woman travelling to the United Kingdom for a termination in August 2016. Travelling with a friend for support, the woman in question turned a private crisis into a powerful political statement, live-tweeting ever stage of her journey to the then-Prime Minister Enda Kenny's Twitter account under the handle #Twowomentravel. #Twowometravel, as mentioned, was picked up by the global media and started trending on Twitter, receiving thousands upon thousands of followers in less than twenty-four hours, including endorsements of solidarity from celebrities worldwide (BBC 2016). The woman's tweets charted how mundane, how ordinary the trip was, from the plane's pre-dawn take-off on a dreary Dublin morning, through to the waiting around in a generic waiting room for the procedure to happen. During this wait the woman inevitably heard the accents of several more Irish women enter and leave the clinic. Some of the women looked scared and apprehensive (Two Women Travel 2016a). Most did not. Afterwards, the woman posted photos of the shabby budget hotel she was staying into Twitter (Two Women Travel

2016b). And the next morning she uploaded a photo of her blood-stained bedsheets after she haemorrhaged during the night following her surgical abortion. A journalist commenting on the story quipped that #Twowomentravel should be renamed #170000womentravel, a reference to the estimated number of Irish women who have had an abortion in the United Kingdom since 1983 (Kelly 2016). Another journalist interviewed the travelling companion as part of #twowomentravel some days after the women had returned home (O'Toole 2016). The travelling companion said of the bold venture:

> What's the alternative? Silence? Silence is breaking 12 Irish hearts a day [the estimated number of Irish women who travel to the UK for a surgical abortion per day]. Silence is trapping migrant women in desperate situations, silence has the blood of Savita on its hands … Silence has devastated the women and girls of Ireland, but now it's time to talk, and get real. (O'Toole 2016, para. 14)

Interestingly, in an early indication of just how influential talking about abortion would be in repealing the Eighth, a number of prominent political figures came out in advance of the campaign to claim that the reason they supported Repeal was a result primarily of the personal testimonies of women they had heard in recent times. Among such figures was the Prime Minister Leo Varadkar. Varadkar had been a long-standing opponent of abortion since he was first elected to public office in 2007, having repeatedly described himself in various government ministries as 'pro-life'. In a 2010 interview with the *Sunday Independent* he said that allowing victims of rape to terminate their pregnancies could give rise to 'abortion on demand', and that while not religious himself he would 'accept a lot of Catholic social thinking' (cited in Ryan 2017, para. 9). On the issue of terminations requested as a result of rape, he added, 'I wouldn't be in favour of it in that case, and, you know, first of all, it isn't the child's fault that they're the child of rape' (cited in Ryan 2017, para. 12). But following the announcement that a referendum on Repeal would be held in summer 2018, pressure grew on the Prime Minister to make his own views known on which side he would be supporting. In a prepared statement in the national parliament, the Dail, on 30 January 2018 Varadkar announced that his position on abortion had now 'evolved' (*Irish Times* 2018a). He explained how, in particular, when he was Minister for Health he had come across instances where women were denied terminations who were in extreme situations of distress, and that this was why he was now supportive of those who wanted to repeal the Eighth. 'In making my decision to support it', he told the Dail, 'I listened to the views of others—medical experts, the public, my party and ministers, friends'. However, the crucial moment in his conversion was when above all, as he stated, 'I listened to women' (*Irish Times* 2018a, para. 3).

Some weeks earlier, the Minister for Health Simon Harris claimed to have experienced a similar about-turn in his own abortion stance. A confessed 'pro-life' politician when he first entered the Dail in 2011, Harris said, 'I came in here thinking that there wasn't a need for change in this country. Genuinely, I didn't believe it' (cited in Doyle 2017, para. 6). However, after meeting several couples who had had a diagnosis of a foetal anomaly in the following years, his outlook began to alter. And, more specifically, the case of Savita Halappanavar weighed on the callow politician. 'I was a young, new, male TD,' Harris said. A TD is the Gaelic abbreviation for *Teachta Dála*, a member or parliament. 'I remember the awful situation with Savita Halappanavar and the real questions that raised about the Eighth Amendment' (cited in Doyle 2017, para. 11).

Most surprisingly, perhaps, Leader of the Opposition Michael Martin was another to credit the direct testimonies of women he had encountered of late as inspiring a volte-face on his own long-held pro-life politics. A member of the Dail since 1989, in a speech in January 2018, Martin said that 'over the years I have been on the record as being against a significant change in our abortion laws' (cited in Fianna Fail 2018, para. 2). But following what he called a 'long period of reflection', his views had departed from this three-decades old stance, and he was now in favour of abolishing the Eighth (Fianna Fail 2018). Martin told the assembled Dail that after seeking out medical opinion, after reading the transcripts of various hearings and written submissions on the Eighth, he had formed the view that there was a 'cruel inflexibility' in the Constitution. Emphatically stating that the Eighth needed to be removed, in forming his newly held view on abortion, Martin concluded, 'Most importantly I have sought to listen to the diverse contributions of women' (cited in Fianna Fail 2018, para. 17).

Indeed, the power of female testimony in altering attitudes towards abortion was to be front and centre in the strategising of the main organisers behind the Repeal campaign, the coalition grouping Together For Yes. After holding a series of focus groups in late 2013 and early 2014, Together For Yes coordinators realised there was still a palpable anger at what had happened to Savita Halappanavar not just in feminist and obviously pro-choice circles but among the general public too (Griffin et al. 2019). Therefore, they concluded that a major plank of their strategy would be to build a campaign around stories not dissimilar to Ms. Halappanavar's. That is, they would concentrate their efforts on the 'hard cases' arising as a result of the Eighth's existence, hoping that such harrowing accounts would sway undecided voters in the upcoming Referendum. As Ailbhe Smyth, joint coordinator for Together For Yes, said, 'From the get-go we were very clear that what would help people was hearing the reality of couples and women who went through very distressing experiences' (cited in Loughlin and O'Cionnaith 2018, para. 22).

With this objective in mind, Communications Director Yvonne Lynch established 'storylab', and set about first gathering and then disseminating first-person testimonies of women's lived experiences under the Eighth Amendment (Griffin et al. 2019). The ambition of this strategy was to create, as Smyth stated, 'a great big behemoth of a campaign based on personal stories' (cited in Loughlin and O'Cionnaith 2018, para. 19). Interestingly, this strategy of placing personal stories at the heart of the campaign was given precedence over and above all other legal, medical, moral, ethical or philosophical argument on abortion. Stories, as Communications Manager Amy Rose Harte put it, were to form a campaign 'spine' that would 'set the tone of the debate' to follow (cited in Loughlin and O'Cionnaith 2018, para. 14).

Together For Yes did receive criticism from certain quarters for this approach. The main accusations against them were that they were disorganised, that they lacked an identifiable figurehead to speak on behalf of the campaign, and that—unlike the No side—they were not assertive enough in getting their message across. Co-director Grainne Griffin refuted this, stating:

> Generally campaigns focus on one or more charismatic individuals to speak for the campaign at all times; our approach was to use a range of people and groups as message carriers. In fact, a lot of the airtime that was counted for the Yes side was interviews with women about their abortion experience without any campaign spokesperson at all. It was interpreted by some as a lack of leadership but actually it was part of our campaign strategy. (Griffin et al. 2019, 161)

Of all these public stories by women of their abortion experience, perhaps the one that caused the loudest controversy came from radio presenter Saoirse Long just two days before polling day. Ms. Long was a guest in the audience of The Pat Kenny Show during the last live head-to-head televised debate in advance of the vote (Griffin et al. 2019). Ms. Long disclosed how in 2014 she had to travel to Birmingham in the United Kingdom to end an unwanted pregnancy. Movingly, she described wandering around a foreign city alone, feeling lost, in considerable physical pain after her surgical procedure, a hot water bottle pressed to her stomach, longing to be at home in bed in Ireland where she could recover. Ronan Mullens, a pro-life senator who was a panellist on the programme and a prominent No campaigner, responded to Ms. Long's revelation by saying, 'Saoirse, you deserve love and respect regardless of what you've ever done' (cited in Larkin 2018, para. 4). Hearing this, Ms. Long was reduced to tears on live television, and there were gasps of disbelief from audience members at Mr. Mullen's apparent lack of empathy for the woman. Viewers of the programme were outraged too, with an incensed response on social media in the wake of the pro-life Senator's remarks. During the broadcast Leo Varadkar took to Twitter to announce that he would be casting a Yes vote on 25 May and that he was doing so 'for all the women in my life, my mum, my sisters, and my female friends, including the friend who told me about her own abortion' (cited in *Irish Examiner* 2018, para. 22).

The foregrounding of female testimony was also the central tactic deployed by the Abortion Rights Campaign (ARC), a core member of the Together For Yes coalition. Throughout 2017 and 2018 the ARC set about hosting a series of 'speak out' sessions at venues up and down the country. The aim of these 'speak-outs' was to help break the silence around abortion in Ireland by encouraging women with actual abortion histories to share their stories in a supportive, intimate and informal environment with others. Pointedly, the ARC stated:

> All year, we hear politicians, media workers and others who call themselves experts talk about a subject they have no direct experience of. This event is entirely dedicated to the voices of abortion seekers of all ages who have been silenced or censored. The Speak Out is an opportunity to connect with experiences like yours and support one another in our everyday attempts to work towards change in Ireland. We do not tell our stories as victims but as survivors and change makers. (Abortion Rights Campaign, 2017, para. 3)

Meanwhile, perhaps reflecting the media habits of a younger generation of women also agitating for legislative change around abortion, a number of online sites dedicated to abortion story-sharing emerged in the wake of the Savita Halappanavar case. The blogging site ShareYourAbortionS tory.tumblr.com was set up in 2013 and began collecting anonymously submitted stories of Irish women who had had abortions and who were passionate that Ireland's laws in this area needed to be changed. With the strapline 'Share Your Experience, Erase The Stigma', the ShareYourAbor-tionStory site received 43 written testimonies of such stories (Share Your Abortion Story 2013). In 2015 and 2016 the SYAS site organisers also hosted writing workshops on how to compose a written abortion story with a non-fiction writing instructor.

Launched in 2015, The X-ile Project shared a similar goal of recording the lived experiences of women affected by the Eighth. However, rather than presenting these experiences as written or verbal testimonies, The X-ile Project consists of a photographic archive of 55 Irish women who have accessed abortion services outside of Ireland. Each photograph is in colour, each taken so that the subject is staring straight into the lens, nothing in silhouette or profile. The Mission Statement of the project is to 'give a much-needed face to those who have been effectively exiled and ignored due to unduly restrictive and oppressive abortion laws' (The X-ile Project 2015). It further seeks to change the nature of the conversation about abortion in Ireland by visibly showing 'those who choose to travel to have an abortion are responsible, ordinary people and are members of our communities' (The X-ile Project 2015). The X-ile Project received extensive press coverage with its photographs being reproduced by major media outlets not only in Ireland but also in the UK, the US, Australia, Belgium, Italy, Poland and France.

Yet another pro-choice initiative to go live on Twitter, Facebook and elsewhere online in the lead-up to the referendum was called Hear Me Out. The aim of Hear Me Out was to get pro-choice voters to have a private conversation about abortion with an undecided voter, and to try to persuade these undecideds why they thought women should have choice when it comes to reproductive matters (Earner-Byrne and Urquhart 2019). Hear Me Out built up to what it termed 'a national day of conversation' on 20 May 2018, and it received widespread attention in the media, as well as numerous endorsements by celebrities, well-known entertainers and politicians. Michelle Darmody, co-founder of Hear Me Out, said, 'I wrote about my own experience of abortion, it was printed in a national newspaper. It made me realise that my story, and everyone else's story, had the power to change peoples' hearts. When something happens to someone you love, it puts it in a very different light' (cited in Hamilton 2018, para. 8). The initiative's Twitter account, #HearMeOut, posted how their Twitter feed had been overwhelmed by the support they had received and 'heartened by the messages telling us how conversations help to encourage yes votes' (cited in Hamilton 2018, para. 19).

Meanwhile, the most prominent of all the online platforms depicting more positive representations of abortion was 'In Her Shoes – Women of the Eighth'. Established in January 2018, 'In her Shoes' is a Facebook page where women can anonymously submit accounts of their abortion experiences (Darcy 2020). Some submissions are just a couple of lines long detailing the circumstances of a pregnancy termination, some reach thousands of words in length. All submissions are anonymous, and each is published alongside a photograph shot from the waist down of a woman wearing a pair of sandals, pumps, heels, boots, slippers, brogues, flipflops and so on. The composition of the photos invites viewers to place themselves 'in her shoes', thereby metaphorically empathising with a woman as she takes the reader on a journey describing how and why she came to have an abortion. The 'In Her Shoes' page had received over 1000 submissions in its first six months. It has a Facebook following of over 100,000 people, and an estimated reader reach of over four-million per week. The social media newswire Storyful claimed the success of 'In Her Shoes' was without question. Monitoring key phrases and hashtags associated with the referendum for a number of months before polling day, Storyful found that 'In Her Shoes' was by far the most successful (Storyful 2018). The page received 640,000 interactions in the month preceding the vote, making it the most interacted-with of all referendum-related Facebook pages by more than double in this period. And like the blogging site ShareYourAbortionStory.tumblr.com, the stories on *In Her Shoes* are a mix of familiar pro-choice 'horror stories' as well as many 'routine abortion' stories.

Indeed, the sheer volume of abortion disclosures appearing into the public domain in advance of the referendum led long-time abortion rights campaigner and Together For Yes co-director Ailbhe Smyth (2018, 127) to remark on just how significantly the public reception of such stories had altered in recent times:

> I'm thinking back to 1992 specifically, because it was very difficult for
> women in 1982 or 1983 to say, 'I had an abortion,' although ... some
> very brave women did, which was really quite extraordinary. I remember
> in 1992 it was particularly international journalists who would come over
> and say, 'We need to speak to women who have had abortions,' and we
> used to say, 'We don't do wombs with a view,' because that's not actually
> what it's about, and that was very much about shielding and protecting
> women who had had abortions.

This time abortion was being debated on air, online and on the ground
in an unprecedented manner. This time a frank, mature discussion of a
crisis pregnancy was possible in Irish public life. This time it was possible
to present 'a womb *with* a view', meaning that Irish women were now
able to come forth and candidly discuss in public the reasons why they
had needed to travel for terminations or clandestinely order abortion pills
online.

In hearing all this it could be argued that a genuine national conversation about abortion was taking place. That a nation of storytellers, if
such a characterisation is in any way accurate, was belatedly taking up a
theme long neglected. And whether they were pro or against Repeal, this
'great big behemoth of a campaign' did show to Irish people at the very
least just how common abortion was in Irish life. And how proximate
too. With all this abortion talk in the air, it was clear abortions weren't
something 'other' women had, 'elsewhere'. Ireland was never 'abortion-
free', as some abortion opponents would like to portray the country. Irish
women had abortions before the Eighth Amendment. They had them
after the Eighth was inserted into the Constitution. And they were going
to continue having them regardless of how the vote went. Abortions were
something all different types of women from all walks of Irish life had. It
could be a procedure the woman sitting on the bus beside you had had.
Or your neighbour down the street. Or the young girl behind the till in
your local shop. It could be a woman who is in employment or unemployed. A student. An immigrant. As easily a doctor as a barista. A waitress
as a barrister. A television presenter. A TD. A woman living on the streets.
It could be your old school friend. Or your old school teacher. Or your
cousin. Or your sister. It could be your mother.

As one woman who was a mother and had ordered abortion pills online
told a radio interviewer, 'I am perfectly normal. I don't have purple hair.
I have never been on a march. I make sandwiches for the GAA' (cited in

Loughlin and O'Cionnaith 2018, para. 29). In describing herself in this manner, this woman was striving to underscore her normalcy. She has a conventional haircut. She is not politically active. She makes refreshments for her local Gaelic Athletic Association team.

And another thing about her—she has had an abortion.

This, too, is part and parcel of her normalcy, her everydayness, her ordinariness.

In disclosing her abortion experience on national radio, this woman contributes to de-stigmatising what remains a discrediting practice in most societies. Stories like hers help de-dramatise abortion talk, moving it from the rhetorical realm of the exceptional and transgressive to the ordinary and mundane. Speaking in this manner helps shift what is medically a routine gynaecological procedure back within the bounds of normative societal behaviour.

Conclusion

While a traditionalist Catholic rump still holds influence in certain spheres of public life in Ireland, in general terms the cultural climate has decisively shifted away from a conservative regime influenced by religious values and a Catholic ethos to one much more tolerant of diverse lifestyles, alternative sexualities, liberal world views (Ferriter 2009; Inglis 2014). A good example of this transition was how, in 2015, the country voted by a landslide to introduce same-sex marriage on a constitutional basis, the first country in the world to so by popular referendum (Tobin 2016). Now, a similar process can be said to have taken place in relation to Ireland's recent Repeal referendum to overturn the country's long-standing ban on abortion provision.

In this chapter I have shown how a key part of, as de Zordo et al. (2016) term it, the 'protest logic' in achieving this outcome was to encourage first-person abortion story-sharing by women. What happened, in effect, was that a sort of normalising of abortion talk took place in the lead-up to the referendum. Here, in unprecedented figures, with unprecedented honesty, women began speaking out about their abortion histories. As mentioned, in most contexts the norm for women remains self-censorship, concealment and non-disclosure of their experiences of terminating an unwanted pregnancy. But in the wake of what happened to Savita Halappanavar in October 2012, something changed. And what changed was that Irish women developed, as Ireland's first Laureate for

Fiction Anne Enright (2018) put it, 'a kind of speech' that allowed them to talk about abortion publicly—what it entailed, why they chose that path, why it was the right decision for them. Enright (2018, para. 11) went on, stating that

> the woman who tells her story becomes Everywoman. She tells a story of inconvenience, difficulty, or outright tragedy and she is made, by her words, powerful. By shaping it in words, a woman possesses an experience that might have possessed her. Making stories brings us outside our own lives and enlarges the experience of our readers. Fellow feeling is a wonderful thing and sympathy works close to joy. These careful accounts, so beautifully told, were the redemptive heart of the Yes campaign.

Rather than that campaign being dominated yet again by the familiar and well-reiterated arguments of pro-choice lawyers, medical experts and politicians, it was the women with real experiences of the procedure who were front and centre in defining the conversation this time. Referring to how the power of personal testimonies had trumped all intellectual arguments both for and against abortion, Enright (2018, para. 19) concluded, 'It was the heart that won – not the gut and not the brain. It was the stories that made the difference.'

It was the stories that made the difference. Echoing Enright, this has been the argument I have elaborated throughout this chapter. The next chapter looks in detail at some of these stories. It considers precisely what pro-choice women with personal experience of abortion had to say on the upcoming Repeal referendum.

References

Abortion Rights Campaign. (2016). *Submission to the citizens assembly.* Available at www.abortionrightscampaign.ie (accessed 1 June 2019).

Abortion Rights Campaign. (2017). *Time to speak out: 2017 Abortion Rights Campaign Speak Out.* Abortion Rights Campaign. Available at https://www.abortionrightscampaign.ie/event/time-to-speak-out-2017-abortion-rights-campaign-speak-out/ (accessed 28 May 2020).

Allen, M. (2014). Narrative diversity and sympathetic abortion: What online storytelling reveals about the prescribed norms of the mainstream movements. *Symbolic Interaction, 38*(1), 42–63.

Allport, G. (1954). *The nature of prejudice.* Reading: Addison-Wesley.

Andeweg, A. (2017). Cultural dimensions of sexual liberalization. *Sexuality & Culture, 21*(2), 339–342.

Armstrong, K. (2019). Together for Yes former co-directors named in TIME 100 list. *Irish Independent.* Available at https://www.independent.ie/irish-news/news/together-for-yes-former-co-directors-named-in-time-100-list-380 24917.html (accessed 28 May 2020).

Baird, B., & Millar, E. (2019). More than stigma: Interrogating counter narratives of abortion. *Sexualities, 22*(7–8), 1110–1126.

BBC. (2016, August 22). *#TwoWomenTravel—Live-tweeting the journey for an abortion.* BBC. Available at https://www.bbc.com/news/blogs-trending-371 56673 (accessed 26 May 2020).

Butler, J. (2016). The horrific court case involving a young pregnant brain-dead woman might not be a one-off. *The Journal.* Available at https://www.thejournal.ie/readme/eight-amendment-abortion-rights-268 5815-Mar2016/ (accessed 28 May 2020).

Carolan, M. (2019). Family of pregnant woman kept on life support gets HSE apology. *Irish Times.* Available at https://www.irishtimes.com/news/crime-and-law/courts/high-court/family-of-pregnant-woman-kept-on-life-support-gets-hse-apology-1.4089935 (accessed 28 May 2020).

Cockrill, K. (2014). Commentary: Imagine a world without abortion stigma. *Women & Health, 54*(7), 662–665.

Cockrill, K., & Biggs, A. (2018). Can stories reduce abortion stigma? Findings from a longitudinal cohort study. *Culture, Health & Sexuality, 20*(3), 335–350.

Connor, D. (2018). Savita Halappanavar's parents call for Yes vote. *RTE.* Available at https://www.rte.ie/news/eighth-amendment/2018/0520/964749-savita-halappanavar/ (accessed 22 June 2018).

Cowan, S. K. (2014). Secrets and misperceptions: The creation of self-fulfilling illusions. *Sociological Science, 1*(2), 466–492.

Cowan, S. K. (2017). Enacted abortion stigma in the United States. *Social Science & Medicine, 177*(4), 259–268.

Cullen, P. (2013). "Horrendous, barbaric, inhumane": Savita's husband gives his verdict. *Irish Times.* https://www.irishtimes.com/news/horrendous-barbaric-inhumane-savita-s-husband-gives-his-verdict-1.1367234 (accessed 28 May 2020).

Darcy, E. (2020). *In her shoes. Women of the Eight: A memoir and anthology.* Dublin: New Island Books.

de Londras, F., & Enright, M. (2018). *Repealing the 8th: Reforming Irish abortion law.* Bristol: Policy Press.

De Zordo, S., Mishtal, J., & Anton, L. (2016). *A fragmented landscape: Abortion governance and protest logics in Europe.* New York: Berghahn Books.

Doyle, K. (2017). Simon Harris: I felt ashamed at abortion treatment and changed my view. *Irish Independent*. Available at https://www.independent.ie/irish-news/politics/simon-harris-i-felt-ashamed-at-abortion-treatment-and-changed-my-view-36443198.html (accessed 15 May 2019).

Earner-Byrne, L., & Urquhart, D. (2019). *The Irish abortion journey, 1920–2018*. London: Palgrave.

Enright, A. (2018). Personal stories are precious things and they made the difference. *Irish Times*. Available at https://www.irishtimes.com/opinion/anne-enright-personal-stories-are-precious-things-and-they-made-the-difference-1.3510189 (accessed 28 May 2020).

Escoffier, J. (Ed.). (2003). *Sexual revolution*. New York: Thunder's Mouth Press.

Ferriter, D. (2009). *Occasions of sin: Sex and society in modern Ireland*. London: Profile Books.

Fianna Fail. (2018). *Speech by Michael Martin on debate on report of Committee on 8th Amendment*. Fianna Fail. Available at https://www.fiannafail.ie/speech-by-micheal-martin-on-debate-on-report-of-committee-on-8th-amendment-18th-jan-2018/ (accessed 1 June 2019).

Fine, G. A. (1995). Public narration and group culture: Discerning discourse in social movements. In H. Johnston & B. Klandermans (Eds.), *Social movements and culture* (pp. 127–143). New York: University of Minnesota Press.

Flynn, T. (2015). You don't talk about abortion in Ireland. But I have to. *Irish Times*. Available at http://www.irishtimes.com/life-and-style/people/tara-flynn-you-don-t-talk-about-abortion-in-ireland-but-i-have-to-1.2344617 (accessed 1 June 2019).

Gentleman, A. (2015). How heartbreak led Helen and Graham Lenihen to campaign for abortion in Ireland. *Guardian*. Available at https://www.theguardian.com/world/2015/oct/19/graham-helen-linehan-ireland-abortion-amnesty-international (accessed 1 June 2019).

Griffin, G., O'Connor, O., Smyth, A., & O'Connor, A. (2019). *It's a yes! How Together for Yes repealed the Eight and transformed Irish society*. Dublin: Orpen Press.

Hamilton, I. (2018). *The hashtag campaign saying 'Hear Me Out' about Ireland's abortion laws*. Mashable. Available at https://mashable.com/2018/05/21/hearmeout-campaign-irish-referendum/?europe=true (accessed 28 May 2020).

Health Services Executive. (2013). *Final report: Investigation of incident 50278 from time of patient's self referral to hospital on 21st of October 2012 to the patient's death on 28th October 2012*. Dublin: HSE.

Herzog, D. (2011). *Sexuality in Europe: A twentieth-century history*. New York: Cambridge University Press.

Holland, K. (2013). *Savita: The tragedy that shook a nation*. Dublin: Transworld Ireland.

Hyland, P. (2012). Youth Defence under investigation over use of image in anti-abortion campaign. *The Journal*. Available at https://www.thejournal.ie/youth-defence-abortion-image-investigation-533369-Jul2012/ (accessed 28 May 2020).

Ingle, R. (2015). Why I need to tell my abortion story. *Irish Times*. Available at http://www.irishtimes.com/life-and-style/people/r%C3%B3is%C3%ADn-ingle-why-i-need-to-tell-my-abortion-story-1.2348822 (accessed 27 May 2019).

Inglis, T. (2014). *Meanings of life in contemporary Ireland: Webs of significance*. London: Palgrave Macmillan.

Irish Examiner. (2018). Taoiseach: Yes in abortion referendum would remove legacy of shame to women. *Irish Examiner*. Available at https://www.irishexaminer.com/breakingnews/ireland/taoiseach-yes-in-abortion-referendum-would-remove-legacy-of-shame-to-women-844919.html (accessed 28 May 2020).

Irish Times. (2018a). Safe, legal and rare: Full text of Taoiseach's abortion speech. *Irish Times*. Available at https://www.irishtimes.com/news/social-affairs/safe-legal-and-rare-full-text-of-taoiseach-s-abortion-speech-1.3373468 (accessed 9 June 2019).

Irish Times. (2018b). Abortion and me: Share your story. *Irish Times*. Available at https://www.irishtimes.com/life-and-style/health-family/abortion-and-me-share-your-story-1.3484457 (accessed 1 June 2019).

Kasstan, B., & Crook, S. (2018). Reproductive rebellions in Britain and the Republic of Ireland: Contemporary and past abortion activism and alternative sites of care. *Feminist Encounters: A Journal of Critical Studies in Culture and Politics, 2*(2), 1–16.

Kelly, C. (2016). TwoWomenTravel should be—170,000 women travel. *Irish Independent*. Available at https://www.independent.ie/opinion/columnists/dr-ciara-kelly-twowomentravel-170000-women-travel-34998798.html (accessed 1 Apr 2019).

Kennedy, J. (2013). Youth Defence billboard posters not covered by advertising standards. *Irish Times*. Available at https://www.irishtimes.com/news/youth-defence-billboard-posters-not-covered-by-advertising-standards-1.954324 (accessed 28 May 2020).

Kimport, K. (2012). (Mis)understanding abortion regret. *Symbolic Interaction, 35*(2), 105–122.

Kumar, A. (2013). Everything is not abortion stigma. *Women's Health Issues, 23*(6), 329–331.

Larkin, L. (2018). "I went number after Mullens' ignorant comment". *The Herald*. Available at https://www.herald.ie/news/i-went-numb-after-mullens-ignorant-comment-long-36944277.html (accessed 28 May 2020).

Loughlin, E., & O'Cionnaith, F. (2018). How they did it: Behind-the-scenes of how the Eighth was repealed. *Irish Examiner*. Available at https://www.iri shexaminer.com/breakingnews/views/analysis/how-they-did-it-behind-the-scenes-of-how-the-eighth-was-repealed-846478.html (accessed 4 May 2019).

Ludlow, J. (2008). The things we cannot say: Witnessing the traumatization of abortion in the United States. *Women Studies Quarterly, 36*(1), 28–41.

Ludlow, J. (2012). Love and goodness: Toward a new abortion politics. *Feminist Studies, 38*(2), 474–483.

Martin, G. (2015). *Understanding social movements*. London: Routledge.

Martin, L. A., Hassinger, J. A., Debbink, M., & Harris, L. H. (2017). Dangertalk: Voices of abortion providers. *Social Science & Medicine, 18*(4), 75–83.

McCarthy, J. (2018). Landslide victory for Yes side in referendum. *RTE*. Available at https://www.rte.ie/news/eighth-amendment/2018/0526/966152-eighth-amendment-referendum/ (accessed 1 Nov 2018).

McDonald, H. (2014). Brain-dead pregnant woman's life support can be switched off, Irish court rules. *Guardian*. Available at https://www.thegua rdian.com/world/2014/dec/26/ireland-court-rules-brain-dead-pregnant-womans-life-support-switched-off (accessed 28 May 2020).

McDonnell, O., & Murphy, P. (2019). Mediating abortion politics in Ireland: Media framing of the death of Savita Halappanavar. *Critical Discourse Studies, 16*(1), 1–20.

McShane, I. (2018). 'Thirty-sixth amendment to the constitution exit poll 25th May, 2018', RTÉ & Behaviour & Attitudes exit poll. Dublin: Behaviour & Attitudes.

Millar, E. (2017). *Happy abortions: Our bodies in the era of choice*. London: Zed Books.

Mullally, U. (Ed.). (2018). *Repeal the 8th*. Dublin: Penguin.

Murray, C. (2016). The protection of life during Pregnancy Act 2013: Suicide, dignity and the Irish discourse on abortion. *Social and Legal Studies, 25*(6), 667–698.

National Women's Council of Ireland. (2012). *Working to improve women's lives: Annual report 2012*. Dublin: NWCI.

O'Brien, J., & Armstrong, K. (2018). It's a big Yes: Stunning victory officially confirmed as 66.4pc vote to reform Ireland's restrictive abortion laws. *Irish Independent*. Available at https://www.independent.ie/irish-news/abortion-referendum/its-a-big-yes-stunning-victory-officially-confirmed-as-66-4pc-vote-to-reform-irelands-restrictive-abortion-laws-36949114.html (accessed 7 May 2019).

O'Carroll, S. (2012, February 6). Twenty years on: A timeline of the X case. *The Journal*. Available at https://www.thejournal.ie/twenty-years-on-a-timeline-of-the-x-case-347359-Feb2012/ (accessed 26 May 2020).

O'Carroll, S. (2018). Savita Halappanavar: Her tragic death and how she became part of Ireland's abortion debate. *The Journal*. Available at https://www. thejournal.ie/eighth-amendment-4-3977441-Apr2018/ (accessed 22 June 2018).

O'Connor, A. (1992). Abortion: Myths and realities from the Irish Folk Tradition. In A. Smyth (Ed.), *The Abortion Papers: Ireland* (pp. 57–65). Dublin: Attic Press.

Polletta, F. (2002). *Freedom is an endless meeting: Democracy in American social movements*. Chicago: University of Chicago Press.

Polletta, F. (2006). *It was like a fever: Storytelling in protest and politics*. Chicago: University of Chicago Press.

Polletta, F., Ching, P., Chen, B., Gharrity Gardner, B., & Motes, A. (2011). The sociology of storytelling. *Annual Review of Sociology, 37*(1), 109–130.

RTE. (2012). Rallies held around Ireland in memory of Savita Halappanavar. *RTE*. Available at https://www.rte.ie/news/2012/1117/346029-vigils-in-dublin-galway-for-savita-halappanavar/ (accessed 11 Jan 2019).

RTE. (2013). Midwife confirms she told Savita Halappanavar Ireland a "Catholic country". *RTE*. Available at https://www.rte.ie/news/health/2013/0410/380613-savita-halappanavar-inquest/ (accessed 1 June 2019).

RTE. (2018). RTE Exit Poll on Eighth Amendment Projects: Yes 69.4% No 30.4%. Available at https://www.rte.ie/news/2018/0525/965899-eighth-amendment/ (accessd 12 May 2020).

RTE. (2019, April 17). Together for Yes co-directors make Time 100 list. *RTE*. Available at https://www.rte.ie/news/ireland/2019/0417/1043182-griffin-smyth-time-list/ (accessed 26 May 2020).

Ryan, P. (2017, October 15). Varadkar defends comments on UK abortion journeys. *Independent*. Available at https://www.independent.ie/irish-news/politics/varadkar-defends-comments-on-uk-abortion-journeys-36227952. html (accessed 26 May 2020).

Share Your Abortion Story. (2013). Available at ShareYourAbortionStory.tumblr. com (accessed 29 May 2020).

Sheridan, K. (2018). Friday is about so much more than abortion. *Irish Times*. Available at https://www.irishtimes.com/opinion/kathy-sheridan-friday-is-about-so-much-more-than-abortion-1.3504515 (accessed 28 May 2020).

Smyth, A. (2018). The obvious explanations of how power is held and exercised over women are very basic. In U. Mullally (Ed.), *Repeal the 8th* (pp. 124–140). Dublin: Penguin.

Specia, M. (2018). How Savita Halappanavar's death spurred Ireland's abortion rights campaign. *New York Times*. Available at https://www.nytimes. com/2018/05/27/world/europe/savita-halappanavar-ireland-abortion.html (accessed 12 June 2019).

Staunton, C. (2011). As easy as A, B and C: Will A, B and C v. Ireland be Ireland's wake-up call of abortion rights? *European Journal of Health Law*, *18*(2), 205–219.

Storyful. (2018). *Ireland's abortion referendum is a test case for democracy.* Storyful. Available at https://storyful.com/resources/blog/how-irelands-abortion-referendum-became-a-test-case-for-democracy-in-the-social-media-age/ (accessed 28 May 2020).

The X-ile Project. (2015). Available at www.x-ileproject.com (accessed 29 May 2020).

Thompson, I. (2018). *How Irish anti-abortion activists are drawing on Brexit and Trump campaigns to influence referendum.* Open Democracy. Available at https://www.opendemocracy.net/en/5050/irish-anti-abortion-campaigners-brexit-trump-data-companies/ (accessed 28 May 2020).

Tobin, B. (2016). Marriage equality in Ireland: The politico-legal context. *International Journal of Law, Policy and the Family, 30*(2), 115–130.

Toole, E. (2016). Abortion in Ireland: "Silence is breaking 12 hearts a day". *Guardian*. Available at https://www.theguardian.com/lifeandstyle/2016/aug/29/abortion-in-ireland-two-women-travel (accessed 26 May 2020).

Two Women Travel. (2016a, August 21). *@endakennyTD forced by more Irish in waiting room.* Twitter. Available at https://twitter.com/twowomentravel?lang=en (accessed 25 May 2020).

Two Women Travel. (2016b, August 21). *Not for the first or the last time a bleeding woman about to face a long treck home.* Twitter. Available at https://twitter.com/twowomentravel?lang=en (accessed 25 May 2020).

Whelan, N. (2012). Decisive change in the abortion debate. *Irish Times.* Available at https://www.irishtimes.com/opinion/decisive-change-in-the-abortion-debate-1.553268 (accessed 7 June 2019).

CHAPTER 4

Repealing the Eighth and Pro-Choice Irish Women's Abortion Testimonies

Abstract This chapter analyses the written abortion testimonies submitted by pro-choice Irish women to the government in advance of the referendum to Repeal the Eighth Amendment in May 2018. These testimonies are all in favour of legal reform to allow abortion access. However, the women's narratives are far from homogeneous in how they present their abortion histories and how they view abortion. Some offer a categorically pro-choice position with unapologetic calls for the liberatory potential of abortion in society to be recognised. Others, however, are far more cautious, far more conciliatory. Here, drawing on a powerful set of normative expectations around femininity, sexuality, class and family, such pro-choice women invoke a particular cultural meaning of abortion that, paradoxically perhaps, calls for the end to prohibitions on abortion while simultaneously provoking certain anti-abortion sentiments in detailing their individual abortion histories.

Keywords Abortion · Pro-choice · Repeal · Republic of Ireland · Written testimonies · Storytelling

INTRODUCTION

One response of pro-choice campaigners in several corners of the world to limited or no abortion service provision has been to encourage personal storytelling by women of their abortion experiences (see Baird and Millar

© The Author(s) 2020

D. Ralph, *Abortion and Ireland*,
https://doi.org/10.1007/978-3-030-58692-8_4

2019; Millar 2017; Pollitt 2014; Thomsen 2013). Aided by a panoply of digital tools and online platforms that extend well beyond the traditional media, lately there has been a proliferation of this mode of confessional public story-sharing around abortion experiences that seeks to expand the repertoire of acceptable abortion stories. Accompanied by images of women seizing bullhorns to roar slogans like 'I Love Abortion' and 'We Love Abortion Providers', a number of social media movements—such as #ShoutYourAbortion, Imnotsorry.net, the 1in3 Campaign, nofilteronline.com, The Abortion Diary and several others—have recently gone 'viral' (Arveda Kissling 2018). Here, women have contributed first-hand abortion accounts to an evolving conversation on what abortion is 'really' like. Many of these story-sharing platforms originated in the United States, though similar movements have sprung up in India ('Voice Your Abortion'), in Australia ('I Had One Too'), in Argentina ('*Que sea ley*', which translates as 'Let It be Law'), in Poland ('*Dziewuchy Dziewuchom*', which translates as 'Gals For Gals'). One recent scholarly investigation into this new-found confidence to discuss abortion issues loudly and non-euphemistically from a pro-choice persuasion titled the resulting monograph *From a Whisper To A Shout* (Arveda Kissling 2018).

The previous chapter has detailed the emergence of this type of first-person abortion story-sharing as a key tactic in the 'protest logics' of pro-choice campaigners in the years and months leading up to the historical Repeal Referendum. It showed how a sort of normalising of abortion talk took place in advance of the referendum, with 'pro-voice' women speaking publicly in unprecedented numbers and with unprecedented candour about their abortion histories. In this, as mentioned, these women storytellers were mirroring certain pro-choice movements in other contexts, where a new 'sound it loud, say it proud' narrative around abortion experiences has emerged in recent years as a central strategy for destigmatising abortion discourse.

What that chapter did not do, however, was to detail what precisely these women's voices actually had to say about abortion. Beyond stating that they were pro-choice and supported amending the current legislation, the last chapter outlined little by way of what being pro-choice entails for women with direct experience of pregnancy termination. In this chapter I analyse these publicly shared accounts of abortion history to consider more closely what being pro-choice might mean.

In this regard, the Republic of Ireland's recent Repeal referendum is a fascinating case. The result of that referendum in May 2018 was an unequivocal mandate for abortion to become legally permissible. As detailed, with over 66 per cent of voters in favour of legal reform allowing abortion provision, commentators variously pronounced how Irish people had at last 'listened to women', how 'women had spoken', how women's 'voices were heard' (RTE 2018). In this chapter I analyse such voices by examining sixty written pro-choice narratives of abortion that were submitted to the government by Irish women as part of the process to hold a referendum on 25 May 2018.

I show how in some of these abortion stories a loudly pro-choice position is advocated, with decibel levels approaching the 'shout' some activists and scholars have recognised among segments of the contemporary transnational pro-choice movement. Such women make unapologetic calls for the liberatory potential of abortion in society to be recognised. At the same time, the abortion stories of these pro-choice women are not always so audible. As often as not, a much more cautious, more conciliatory pro-choice stance is taken, expressed in a voice at times closer to a 'whisper'. Here, drawing on a powerful set of normative expectations around femininity, sexuality, class and family, such pro-choice women invoke a particular cultural meaning of abortion that, paradoxically perhaps, calls for the end to prohibitions on abortion while simultaneously provoking certain anti-abortion sentiments in detailing their individual abortion histories. Overall, these women's pro-choice written testimonies suggest a stance, to paraphrase Arveda Kissling (2018), 'between a whisper and a shout' rather than the more unequivocal 'from a whisper to a shout' her research into abortion activist found.

Representing Abortion: The Social Meanings of Abortion

Public attitudes towards abortion vary considerably from country to country. That said, a recent YouGov-Cambridge Globalism survey found a general tend whereby in wealthier countries, much more accepting views on abortion are prevalent while in poorer countries the procedure continues to be viewed with widespread societal disapproval (Duncan et al. 2019). The United States, however, was an outlier in this overall pattern for wealthier countries, with more Americans opposed to than supportive of abortion. In fact, with 46 per cent of Americans finding abortion to be 'very unacceptable', US opposition levels towards abortion were closer to those found in Turkey at 47 per cent and India at 48 per cent (Duncan et al. 2019).

Yet despite these fluctuating public attitudes on pregnancy terminations, in much popular Western culture abortion continues to occupy the status of a taboo (Martin et al. 2017). On the rare occasions when the subject is addressed in film, television, magazines or novels, it is mostly done so through the lens of a limited set of representational stereotypes that, in many instances, do not reflect the 'real life' experience of pregnancy terminations (Sisson and Kimport 2014). Almost unanimously, these stereotypes frame abortion as an exceptionally 'difficult decision' for any woman to make, while the experience itself is inevitable understood as 'traumatic', 'stigmatizing', 'transgressive', an 'exceptional life event' (Beynon-Jones 2017; Cockrill and Nack 2013; Condit 1990; Kimport 2012; Ludlow 2012). There is in most depictions of the medical procedure what Hadley (1997) calls the persistent 'awfulization' of abortion, after which, as night follows day, the aborting woman will undergo a bout of 'post-abortion syndrome' comprising crippling regret over the loss of her potential child, or what Millar (2017) calls 'foetocentric grief'. As a consequence, the available social discourses to discuss, debate and interpret abortion in most Western societies remain extremely restricted—including societies where abortion is legally permissible—and the routinised ways in which women can talk about the procedure highly circumscribed (Sanger 2017). Typically such socially legitimate abortion talk involves women assuming a sacrificial stance whereby their decision to end a pregnancy is justified as a 'good' abortion if it relates not to any direct personal or career reasons but more to that of potential future children or already existing children (Lowe 2016; Lowe and Page 2018). Conversely, a 'bad' abortion involves one where a woman acts primarily out of self-interest (Baird 1998).

But given the broad spectrum of human emotions, some activists and abortion researchers have asked recently why so remarkably few ever seem to be drawn upon when discussing abortion. For instance, Millar (2017), considering the politics of abortion in Australia, argues the reason the affective landscape of abortion is so impoverished is because of the ongoing negative cultural meanings attached to it in most societies. There seems to be a silent contract that in exchange for legally sanctioned abortions, women in the Western world must internalise stigmatised identities that, in Kumar et al.'s (2009, 628) influential definition, 'marks them, internally or externally, as inferior to ideals of womanhood'. Further, as part of this silent contract, aborting women must remain silent about their experiences while expressing sadness and sorrow over a lost foetus (Lupton 2013; Millar 2016; Petchesky 1987). They must be, in short, both troubled and apologetic about their abortions. Referring specifically to the United States, this is of a piece with what Weitz (2010, 168) calls the 'mantra' popularised by Bill Clinton in the 1990s that abortions should only be 'safe, legal and rare', which, as she argues, may in fact run counter to and be 'ineffective as a strategy for securing rights'. To suggest that abortion should be 'rare' is to suggest it be restricted, is to suggest it be rationed, is to suggest all measures be taken to reduce its incidence. In fact, this framing of abortion as legally permissibly yet discouraged is tantamount, as Weitz (2010, 168) underscores, to making it a 'non-normative practice that is unworthy of societal approval'.

Why this disapproval? Why this distaste? Is it not possible that abortion could be seen as a life-affirming, transformative and positive event in some women's lives? Could abortion be, in some situations, not a soul-searchingly, deeply existential decision but an obvious one, a practical option? By calling for women to be more frank about their abortion experiences, these activists hope to 'normalise' it, showing that abortions are, for the most part, untroubling, unexceptional, non-traumatic (Belfrage et al. 2019; Filipovic 2016; Kumar 2013). What these discursive interventions can do is shape the dialogue on abortion so as to encourage more support for a pro-choice orientation (Allen 2014). By mobilizing a counter-narrative to dominant modes of representation of abortion, they help open up a discursive space wherein the decision to terminate a pregnancy may be spoken about unapologetically (Millar 2017). It creates the possibility to hear non-defensive, non-stigmatised abortion stories as potentially celebratory acts rather than the familiar images of doom that the word 'abortion' incites in many (Cockrill 2014; Cockrill and Biggs 2018; Freedman and Weitz 2012). Indeed, this chimes with the findings of studies carried out in the United States and the United Kingdom into women's mental health difficulties post-abortion, which find no correlation between women's abortion history and any acute, long-term mental health problems (Cameron 2010; Greene Foster 2020; Lee 2003, 2017; Major et al. 2009; Rocca et al. 2015).

The recent surge of alternative voices demanding there be, as Pollitt (2014) terms it, 'no more apologies' around abortions suggests a shift may be underway in the ways in which the procedure is framed, discussed and represented in cultural narratives. In other words, the discursive hegemony that anti-abortionists have enjoyed in the abortion debate may be beginning to weaken, to be challenged. However, as Baird and Millar (2019) state, this shift has not necessarily been adequately addressed in abortion scholarship yet. With some significant exceptions mentioned here, there is a significant scholarly gap analysing pro-choice viewpoints that do not default to the 'awfulization' of abortion as a 'difficult decision' followed by inevitable psychological trauma, guilt, stigma, regret, and so on.

In this chapter I contribute to recent abortion scholarship that seeks to address this gap. I analyse first-person written testimonies of Irish women who have experienced abortion to do so. First, however, I outline the qualitative analytic methods through which I sourced, analysed and interpreted these testimonies.

METHODOLOGY

In 2016, the Abortion Rights Campaign (ARC) made a call for women directly affected by the Eighth Amendment to contribute their written abortion testimonies to be included as part of the ARC's official submission to the Citizen's Assembly on the abortion issue (Abortion Rights Campaign 2016). As discussed in the previous chapter, the ARC was one of the main pro-choice advocacy organisations behind the success of the Repeal movement. Alongside the National Women's Council and the Irish Family Planning Association, the ARC was one of three core groups to form the large-scale civil society umbrella coalition Together For Yes (Griffin et al. 2019). The ARC's aims are to engage in community education to facilitate 'stigma-busting' around abortion, to ensure public visibility of pro-choice positions in the media, and to contribute to policy work that ensures abortion is not just 'safe, legal and rare' as the Prime Minister Leo Varadkar advocated during the Referendum campaign (Irish Times Irish Times 2018), but is rather 'free, safe and legal' for all who need it, 'regardless of citizenship or financial capacity, in line with provision of other basic healthcare options' (Abortion Rights Campaign 2016, 4).

The Citizen's Assembly is composed of one-hundred randomly selected citizens who make recommendations to the Government on matters of pressing sociopolitical importance. The ARC's submission to them contained 60 first-person written testimonies from women who had experienced abortion. The ARC (2016, 5) stated that it hoped the testimonies would help 'to start a discussion about abortion … a national conversation about why women seek and obtain abortions, what happens when women do not have access to safe abortion, and how abortion should be provided'. These testimonies are freely available to consult on the Citizen's Assembly's website (https://www.citizensassembly.ie/en/Submissions/Eighth-Amendment-of-the-Constitution/Submissions-Received/). Based on the submissions received by the closing date of 16 December 2016, the Assembly was tasked then with making an official recommendation to the Government on how to proceed. In April 2017, Assembly members voted 79 to 12 in favour of holding a referendum on the Eighth, and eleven months later the Government announced that this referendum would take place on 25 May 2018 (McGreevy 2018). The ARC's submission of 60 written abortion testimonies contributed to this decision to hold a referendum on the Eighth.

Between January 2019 and March 2019 I carried out a thematic content analysis of these testimonies from a feminist theoretical stance (Reinharz and Davidman 1992). The ARC (2016, 29) state that the testimonies they received were not edited: 'We have not edited them. These are their [women's] words, as they told them'. However, as all the written submissions contain no identifying information about particular individuals and the document itself appears to have undergone a rigorous spellcheck before being submitted, it can be assumed that individual testimonies have in fact been anonymised, as well as proofed for minor typographical errors. Further, when the ARC made the call for women's testimonies to be included as part of its Government submission it is possible that they may have received some anti-choice testimonies. The ARC, as the prime pro-choice lobby group in Ireland, is likely to have excluded such anti-choice testimonies in its own submission, if it received such. This should be minded when considering the analysis that follows below.

As for the actual testimonies themselves submitted by the ARC, they varied in length, the shortest being just under 400 words, the longest 6344. The ARC offered a series of prompt questions to help women compose their testimonies. Some women answered each of the prompts in putting together their testimony. Others ignored them and instead wrote a direct account of their abortion histories under the Eighth Amendment. The coding of the testimonies followed a two-step process. Step 1 involved an open coding process whereby I discovered substantive themes emerging across the submissions. Step 2 involved a more focussed coding process, refining the core emergent concepts around 'positive' and 'negative' abortion portrayals. These refined codes then guided my subsequent analysis and interpretation.

Taken together, the 60 testimonies represent a powerful primary source of extant qualitative data on abortion in Ireland. While the testimonies were not explicitly produced for the purposes of research, their format may in fact be more advantageous than that of traditional qualitative data collection methods like in-depth interviews and focus groups (Reinharz and Davidman 1992). As abortion in any context is a deeply private issue, collating women's thoughts, feelings and views on their personal abortion histories via written submission may be a more unobtrusive and productive way of eliciting meaningful responses to the subject than via the spoken word (Silverman 2001). A researcher's presence in a face-to-face format discussing a topic like abortion could potentially hinder respondents' accounts, particularly a male researcher like myself (Dickson-Swift et al. 2007). As such, written submissions like those discussed in this paper allow women to take their time in composing their own narratives, in their own words.

Of course a limitation of such material is that it assumes a certain level of literacy on the behalf of women who produce them. Issues of representativeness necessarily arise here, as such accounts exclude those with literacy issues. The testimonies analysed below are biased in that they are the product of individuals who are all highly literate, highly articulate, and possessing a high level of general education. This too should be kept in mind when considering the various discursive framings of abortion reflected in these pro-choice portrayals of personal abortion history.

PRO-CHOICE WOMEN'S WRITTEN FIRST-PERSON TESTIMONIES

Throughout the sixty written testimonies the notion of compulsory motherhood is anathema to all of the women. That a government could, through its laws, effectively conscript women into delivering children they do not want is seen as a long-standing societal injustice that must be overcome. A number stated clearly that the idea of enforced pregnancy is a form of torture, and said that they were not incubators or vessels for reproduction for the Irish state. Almost all noted, too, how privileged or lucky they were in being able to travel outside the state for a termination. They were aware that without the necessary financial, emotional and logistical support they had they may have been forced to carry an unwanted pregnancy to term. Here they contrasted their situations with those of women in more vulnerable or disadvantaged situations such as asylum seekers and others living in extreme poverty. As noted, all are in favour of overturning the constitutional restrictions imposed on women by the 1983 Eighth Amendment that made abortion illegal in the vast range of circumstances. However, the voices of these pro-choice women are far from uniform in their depictions of abortion. As the analysis that follows underscores, two main thematic issues emerged, with more 'positive' portrayals of abortion on the one hand, more 'negative' on the other.

Abortion as a Simple, Positive Decision, or Towards the Possibility of a Happy Abortion

Of the 60 pro-choice submissions analysed, 29 testimonies were categorised as offering an optimistic appraisal of abortion and their own personal abortion histories. The main codes reiterated across this set of narratives included an unapologetic recounting of a pregnancy termination alongside calls for a more emancipatory feminist politics that sees abortion access as fundamental to female reproductive justice. Here, as in other research on abortion 'decisional rightness' (Rocca et al. 2015), women see the decision to cease being unwillingly pregnant as a straightforward one to make and report few if no feelings of remorse or regret post-abortion. Often, what is foregrounded is a sense of relief and even elation that they did not have to become mothers against their will. Availing themselves of an abortion allowed these women to pursue goals other than motherhood. For this a number felt gratitude and could subsequently articulate positive identities in relation to their abortion decision.

Several were convinced that the moment they learned they were pregnant they knew instantly, even in the very second they made the discovery, that they would not be going ahead with the pregnancy. There was nothing troubling about making the choice to continue the pregnancy or not. There was no breast beating. They were unapologetic about that. For instance, one woman stated that she was certain of her decision to end her pregnancy from the start and never once cast doubt on the path ahead of her. For these reasons, she claimed, it was easy to avail of an early termination. She went on, explaing that she was not in any way ashamed of the fact that she had an abortion. It was what was necessary, she said, for her at that time in her life. What was shaming, she went further, was that she had to live in a country with a government that insisted she lie about her abortion and hide the fact of her abortion history, which caused the termination to feel much more serious than it needed to be.

A second woman echoed this sentiment, writing that while she did regret aspects of the situation, she in no way regretted her decision. She said she felt disappointed that her government failed to recognise her capacity as a mature adult woman to make responsible choices that impact on both her partner's life and her own.

Another woman placed the decision to abort an unwanted pregnancy on par with contraceptive failure and her subsequent actions were about rectifying that failure. Writing how having an abortion was not something she ever blamed herself for or felt guilty about, she stated that the thing she did regret was that the condom broke and that she didn't quite think through the likelihood of getting pregnant in that particular instance.

Meanwhile, the following woman forthrightly located any fault arising from her abortion not with herself but with the country's antiquated legislative regime around women's reproductive rights. She pointed out in her testimony that she will not be made to feel shame for her decision to end an unwanted pregnancy because of Ireland's misogynistic and outmoded laws. She went on to state unequivocally that she is a person who deserves to determine what happens to her body and her life.

Several women attested to few or even no negative emotions arising as a result of their abortions. For example, stating that she was strongly pro-choice, one woman's submission outlined how she had had two abortions, and had never once regretted either of them or had any misgivings. Echoing this sentiment, another woman said she had zero regret, that it was without question the best thing for her and her family. She elaborated on this point, saying how she thought abortion was a healthcare issue that should be available to anyone who needs it, preferably with the help and support of the country in which they live. She went further, not just experiencing an absence of 'hurt' but instead framed her actions in positive terms: she claimed, all in all, she was so happy, so relieved that she was able to have an abortion when she needed one.

A second woman shared this position when she wrote that she had never regretted her abortion and was happy she had made that decision. In a similarly assured vein, another woman insisted she experienced a sense of euphoria in the abortion clinic even while bleeding heavily after the surgical procedure, while another said she felt empowered in the choice she had made. Yet another said the relief she experienced after her abortion was spectacular, while the procedure itself was mundane, not at all traumatic. Meanwhile, the woman describing herself as strongly pro-choice who had had two abortions added that morally, emotionally, ethically, she never regretted a solitary thing about it. She reiterated the point: she is a well-educated, well-balanced adult who has never regretted her choices. Those choices, rather, are all a part of what makes her who she is.

Here, countering the widespread 'awfulization' of the procedure, these women are wresting back some of the representational terrain around which abortion debates endlessly circle (Dadlez and Andrews 2010; Kelly 2014). Far from the many contraindications often associated with the procedure—loss, grief, regret, trauma—the testimonies analysed in this section underscored the affirming, positive aspects of their decision to not continue carrying an unwanted pregnancy gave them. Such voices are a crucial intervention in abortion debates, as they begin to shift the overwhelmingly negative discursive stereotypes that have long dominated most abortion talk towards more positive—and, it should be added, realistic—representations of what abortion is 'really like'. As Pollitt (2014) argues, it is not that abortion is not talked about. Sometimes, referring specifically to the American context but one that in many ways reflects the Irish context too, she suggests it seems like people talk about little else. The problem, however, is the *way* abortion is debated, and this includes the way pro-choice advocates speak about the issue with a distinctly 'apologetic rhetoric'. In the ongoing struggle to secure women's reproductive rights, Pollitt (2014) has called for an alternative to this way of talking about abortion, one that is forthright, candid, and above all, unrepentant. The women's written testimonies analysed in this section reflect this alternative way of talking about abortion. As such, their voices proffer what Millar (2017) suggests remains all but 'unsayable'—that is, the possibility of a 'happy abortion'.

Abortion as an Agonizing Decision, or Recuperating Maternity Femininity Within a Pro-Choice Logic

A second set of 31 narratives were classified as consisting of a non-normative interpretation of abortion. Here, a series of codes continually appeared in the written accounts that presented a cultural framing of abortion as a deeply stigmatising, non-normative practice. Feelings of guilt and regret over a lost foetus were evident in several, while abortion itself was routinely understood not as a repudiation of motherhood per se but more as a means of securing the ideal of middle-class motherhood in the future. In other words, abortion in these accounts is not in and of itself condoned but becomes socially acceptable when framed as the best way of achieving normative maternal femininity at a later stage in their reproductive lifespans. What emerges is a discourse around abortion that understands the decision itself as an agonising, heartbreaking one that is ultimately justified as acting in the best interests of responsible (future) maternity over and above selfish individual preferences in the present.

Take this woman, whose sentiment was shared across numerous accounts. She said that, for her, choosing to have an abortion was an extremely difficult decision to arrive at, and one she considered long and hard. She knew, in the end, that terminating her pregnancy was the correct choice for her, but she stressed that it was not a responsibility she ever took lightly. Another woman echoed this, and remarked that abortion is never something that is fashionable or a badge of honour.

References to how freighted with doubts, fears and hesitations the decision to have an abortion was reoccurred throughout the testimonies here. And in the process, many were at pains to place themselves at a remove from the stereotype of the 'selfish aborting woman' (Baird 1998), underscoring over and over how it was precisely the opposite of a narcissistic, frivolous decision: it was weighty, burdensome, only arrived at after protracted and intense deliberation.

The following woman's account reflects this circular, distressing process. She claimed that her partner is a slower decision-maker than her, that he needed more time than her to think about what they could do. She knew from what he said, or more to the point from what he didn't say, that he had difficulty with abortion. She wrote about how they would talk together in bed at night, talk about what they might do about having the abortion or not. They did this over and over. She wrote how they cried over and over too. If the point needed emphasising, she added that for anyone who thinks abortion is a decision made lightly, they'd be wrong. Completely wrong.

The woman went on to describe her confusion, explaining how she eventually became so agitated she felt like she was almost suffocating on her indecision. She spoke to what she referred to as the baby in bed at night, trying to figure out the right thing to do, the correct course of action. She grew disconsolate. She tried with her partner to imagine a scenario where they could make the whole situation work. But in the end, she stated, she'd be brought back with a bang to the fact that they didn't even have a roof to put over their heads, let alone any of the other essentials a child would need.

She got the abortion in the United Kingdom.

She repeated her insistence that the main reason for this was that she could not give the child the life it deserves. It was the basics she kept returning to. Housing. Health care. Food. She concluded by writing that she had put her own feelings aside in an endeavour to decide what was best for the potential child, and she was sure that was it.

In insisting that she somehow bracketed her own feelings in an effort to prioritise the interests of the potential child, this woman's account clearly reflects what Millar (2017) calls the socially hegemonic pro-choice narrative that is not simply 'pro-choice' but specifically 'maternal pro-choice'. A maternal pro-choice position, Millar argues, is avowedly *not* pro-abortion, an act that is understood generally as 'distasteful' even if it is inevitable. Millar identifies a thriving maternal pro-choice scholarly literature that repeatedly frames abortion as a 'bad thing' for women at the same time as it admits abortion access to be a necessary right of women. Drawing on arguments presented in *The Abortion Myth* (Cannold 1998), *Not An Easy Choice* (McDonnell 1984), *The Ambivalence of Abortion* (Francke 1978) and other influential texts, Millar shows how a maternal pro-choice logic is achieved, first, by privileging the status of the foetus in imaginings of pregnancy and, second, erasing the subject position of the unwillingly pregnant women from the abortion decision itself. With this twofold manoeuver, then, the view can be put forward that abortion is an act of selfless maternal sacrifice undertaken with the primary aim of securing the wellbeing of could-be children. Lowe (2016, 119) agrees with this, stating, '"proper" women are expected to put the welfare of children, whether born, *in utero*, or not yet conceived over and above any choice or desires of their own'.

Often running alongside this maternal pro-choice stance which justifies ending an unwanted pregnancy more for selfless than selfish reasons is a normative ideal of middle-class femininity that sees young women as in preparation for their future role of motherhood. They prepare for this role by finding the right partner, attaining sufficient social capital and educational qualifications, then securing stable careers so as not to become burdens on the welfare system once they enter motherhood. Paradoxically, perhaps, their abortions are made meaningful by foregrounding their maternal identities; their decision to terminate a pregnancy in the past is linked directly to their future desire to attain, to paraphrase Lowe (2016), 'proper motherhood'.

This normative framing of femininity as achieving proper motherhood is captured in the following woman's account. She stated that if pro-life advocates had their way then she would be pregnant right now with a child she does not want, in a relationship that is not prepared for a child, and in a life where she would be depressed because she would have had to give up her career while going on a waiting list for social housing and living off the meagre social welfare provisions provided by the state. So, in trying to protect the unborn child, the woman stated, pro-life proponents force people into poverty and mental illness. How, the woman asked, does that help the unborn child other than the fact that it is alive?

In possibly the most direct testimony to re-inscribe abortion into a robust expression of maternal identity, one woman made a direct connection between the abortion she had three years earlier, and the subsequent birth of her beloved son. Without her trip to the United Kingdom for a legal and safe abortion, her son, she wrote, would simply not have been born. Her relationship, she was sure, with her son's father would have ended much earlier without the earlier abortion, and therefore her son would never have been conceived.

Similarly, in detailing an abortion some years previously, this woman was careful to emphasise how her termination was not about a repudiation of motherhood per se but merely its deferral until the right circumstances materialised to allow her to mother in the manner she saw most appropriate—at the right time, with the right partner, in the right milieu. Becoming a mother at that earlier moment in her life rather than later would, she suggested, have undermined her future employment prospects and chances of independence by jeopardising her education. So she chose not to create a child at that time. She wrote how she could not see how this was not the most responsible approach to parenting. Yet, she went on, she finds her decision being derided by pro-life people who profess to love and care for the welfare of children and families.

Further, she pointed out that while some people might see hers as a socially discrediting 'elective' or 'convenience' or 'lifestyle' abortion, in fact she understood her own actions ultimately not as callous or selfish but as an instance of 'responsible maternity'. She wrote how even though she felt stigmatised for aborting she also felt that this was by far the most responsible thing to do given her situation. Sometimes, she stated, she encountered circumstances like her own described negatively as 'social' abortions. Yet, she asked, don't we as a society place most value on any person or couple's realistic assessment of their financial, emotional and psychological conditions as the very social factors that should influence when and how they bring children into the world?

Abortion here is seen as a legitimate option in that it is undertaken within an emotional economy directed towards gathering the necessary resources to protect and guarantee the happiness of future children, could-be children, potential children. If it were undertaken for other reasons, reasons that could be classified as more selfish, it would be deemed illegitimate is the implication behind these testimonies.

These 'maternal pro-choice' accounts form a sort of 'abortion common sense', setting the parameters of acceptable and unacceptable abortions. As Lowe (2016, 119) states, 'good abortions' are ones that postpone motherhood until such time as a woman can 'put any child's interests first' whereas 'bad abortions' are ones where women put their own lives 'above that of the foetus and thus fail to act as appropriate women'. Such accounts also echo Ginsburg and Rapp's (1995) influential concept of 'stratified reproduction'—the idea that fertility should be promoted in certain women while prevented in others. In the previous testimony, responsibility is underscored as key to the decision to become a mother; the responsible thing to do is to postpone her reproductive career until such time as adequate socio-economic resources can be mobilised to support a child. Conversely, the 'irresponsible thing' which clearly marks some (working-class) women's reproductive choices is to become mothers to children they cannot financially or emotionally support.

The following woman's account encapsulates every aspect of this maternal pro-choice viewpoint. She wrote how she has always wanted children, has in fact always wanted a large family. But, she asked, how could she possibly discontinue her education, when she had so much more to do? How could she be expected to provide for a child without a degree, and to go from the relative safety of a medical career, to none at all? She was an older student, she went on, when she commenced her course, having taken a couple of years out of formal education. So she was already behind most of her school friends when she started university, who were by now in salaried employment. How could she fall even further behind? she wrote. She said that she knew parents of young children and was fully aware of the demands, stresses and sacrifices that are involved with parenting. Not only did she know she was not equipped to handle the emotional stress, she also could not financially afford a child. She found out what financial assistance was available to young mothers still in college, if creche places were financed, but the subsidies on offer still meant a monthly expense equivalent to more than two months of her salary. Her partner was also a student, with massive debt. These, she stated categorically, were the facts, this was the reality of her and her partner's situation. No amount of words, or pity, or wishful thinking that things would simply work out, she went on, would change any of this. There was no choice but one, she said, and it was the right choice for her, for her partner, and for any future children she might go on to have.

This woman explicitly postpones motherhood until such time as she has amassed the social and economic capital necessary to support a child in a middle-class environment. She recuperates herself to socially acceptable norms of femininity by insisting the decision to abort her pregnancy was not a merely selfish one undertaken with herself in mind primarily. Rather, invoking the welfare of others, including the 'future children' she may go on to have, was the key determinant behind her termination. This account aligns perfectly with normative discursive framings of what is 'sayable' in the present (neoliberal) political moment about abortion in many Western contexts (Katz and Tirone 2015; Solinger 2013). This woman's abortion was not a rejection of motherhood in itself but rather its deferral until such time as she can become a 'good' maternal subject— that is, embedded in a stable heterosexual partnership equipped with the requisite educational, social and economic clout to be self-sufficient and independent of state subventions.

Conclusion

Given the restrictive interpretative repertoire available to women to discuss, debate and understand abortion in most contexts, it is not surprising that in recent years a counter-narrative to hegemonic discursive framings of the procedure have arisen. Here, what scholars, activists and individual women with experience of abortion have attempted to counter is the widespread 'awfulization' of abortion by wresting back some of the representational terrain around which abortion debates endlessly circle. And, indeed, the analysis above has shown that invoking the possibility of emotionally benign abortions is a possibility for some. Far from assuming the common sense stance that abortion must be a torturously difficult decision to make followed by the most horrendous psychological sequelae, almost half the written testimonies infuse the procedure with more positive interpretations and more celebratory emotions. Abortion here is presented not inevitably as a life-altering incident but rather as something routine, mundane, a decision that was simple. And in place of the guilt that is commonly attributed to the aftermath of the procedure, so absent was this in in many that they claimed the only actual guilt they felt was for feeling no guilt whatsoever about their abortion(s). Rather, their overriding emotion was relief.

That said, a second pro-choice stance was equally dominant in the analysis of the written testimonies presented above. In these accounts a sort of 'pro-choice-but-anti-abortion' middle ground was presented that at once framed the procedure as non-normative while also calling for a lifting of legal prohibition against abortion access. Reflecting what Millar (2017) calls a maternal pro-choice logic, a relatively circumscribed set of discursive figures are drawn upon in these pro-choice narratives whereby aborting women describe both the lead-up to the procedure and its aftermath as one in which maternal sacrifice is articulated, reiterated and invoked. Here, the decision to end an unwanted pregnancy is routinely depicted as one of great enormity, justified not in terms of women's self-determination or self-centredness but rather about keeping the best interests of already born or potential future children in mind. They normalise a middle-class ideal of motherhood as a course of action that should be pursued, but only at the right time, with the right person, in the right social, emotional and financial circumstances. Barring this, abortion is a viable option.

Taken together, then, these pro-choice written testimonies do not explicitly represent abortion as something that should be an unconditional part of women's reproductive rights and health care. While all the testimonies are pro-choice, at the same time pregnancy termination in several accounts is couched in numerous qualifications, and far from any full-throated, ringing endorsement of the procedure what comes across most forcefully in fact is a sort a defensive, almost apologetic justification of abortion access. Or, to paraphrase Arveda Kissling (2018) once more, instead of Irish pro-choice women's written testimonies to the Government in support of removing the Eighth Amendment from the Constitution shifting 'from a whisper to a shout' a more accurate portrayal of their abortion advocacy is that of being caught somewhere 'between a whisper and a shout'.

In the next and final chapter I develop this argument, showing how adopting such an in-between position may have significant anti-abortion side-effects in restricting women's future access to reproductive rights. I argue that taking this somewhat tepid pro-choice position may be what 'hurts women' in the long term insofar as it allows anti-choice campaigners to gain ground in winning discursive arguments to restrict or erode abortion access. To ensure this does not happen it is important for pro-choice advocates to be more vocal in presenting their case for women's rights to reproductive autonomy. Referring specifically to the rollback of abortion services in the United States in the decades since the 1973 Roe v. Wade ruling that first legalised abortion there, Katha Pollitt (2014, 41) states: 'Forty years of apologetic rhetoric, forty years of searching for arguments that will support legal abortion while never, ever implying that it is an easy decision or a good thing—for women, men, children, families, society—have left the pro-choice movement making the same limited, defensive arguments again and again'. Such limited, defensive arguments, I outline in what follows, grants abortion opponents the impetus in defining the terms of the 'abortion debate'. One way of defending against this is to create a space for discussing abortion as a force for moral and social good. This, I detail, calls for developing a culture of outspokenness around abortion as a key strategy in countering further anti-abortion inroads into women's reproductive lives.

References

Abortion Rights Campaign. (2016). *Submission to the citizens assembly*. Available at www.abortionrightscampaign.ie (accessed 1 June 2019).

Allen, M. (2014). Narrative diversity and sympathetic abortion: What online storytelling reveals about the prescribed norms of the mainstream movements. *Symbolic Interaction, 38*(1), 42–63.

Arveda Kissling, E. (2018). *From a whisper to a shout: Abortion activism and social media*. London: Repeater Books.

Baird, B. (1998). *"Somebody was going to disapprove anyway": Re-thinking histories of abortion in South Australia*. Ph.D. dissertation, Flinders University.

Baird, B., & Millar, E. (2019). More than stigma: Interrogating counter narratives of abortion. *Sexualities, 22*(7–8), 1110–1126.

Belfrage, M., Ortíz Ramírez, O., & Sorhaind, A. (2019). Story circles and abortion stigma in Mexico: A mixed-methods evaluation of a new intervention for reducing individual level abortion stigma. *Culture, Health and Sexuality, 1*, 96–111.

Beynon-Jones, S. M. (2017). Untroubling abortion: A discourse analysis of women's accounts. *Feminism & Psychology, 27*(2), 225–242.

Cameron, S. (2010). Induced abortion and psychological sequelae. *Best Practice & Research Clinical Obstetrics & Gynaecology, 24*(5), 657–665.

Cannold, L. (1998). *The abortion myth: Feminism, morality, and the hard choices women make*. New York, NY: Wesleyan University Press.

Cockrill, K. (2014). Commentary: Imagine a world without abortion stigma. *Women & Health, 54*(7), 662–665.

Cockrill, K., & Biggs, A. (2018). Can stories reduce abortion stigma? Findings from a longitudinal cohort study. *Culture, Health & Sexuality, 20*(3), 335–350.

Cockrill, K., & Nack, A. (2013). "I'm not that type of person": Managing the stigma of having an abortion. *Deviant Behaviour, 34*(12), 973–990.

Condit, C. (1990). *Decoding abortion rhetoric: Communicating social change*. Chicago, IL: University of Illinois Press.

Dadlez, E. M., & Andrews, W. L. (2010). Post-abortion syndrome: Creating an affliction. *Bioethics, 24*(9), 445–452.

Dickson-Swift, V., James, E. L., Kippen, S., & Liamputtong, P. (2007). Doing sensitive research: What challenges do qualitative researchers face? *Qualitative Research, 7*(3), 327–353.

Duncan, P., Glenza, J., & Rice-Oxley, M. (2019). US more anti-abortion than other developed countries—Global poll. *Guardian*. Available at https://www.theguardian.com/world/2019/may/17/us-more-anti-abortion-than-other-developed-countries-global-poll (accessed 21 Nov 2019).

Filipovic, J. (2016). With Pro Katha Pollitt gives the abortion rights movement its modern credo. *Signs: Journal of Women in Culture and Society, 41*(4), 979–999.

Francke, L. B. (1978). *The ambivalence of abortion*. New York, NY: Penguin Books.

Freedman, L., & Weitz, T. A. (2012). The politics of motherhood meets the politics of poverty. *Contemporary Sociology, 20*(1), 36–42.

Ginsburg, F., & Rapp, R. (1995). *Conceiving the new world order: The global politics of reproduction*. Berkeley, CA: University of California Press.

Greene Foster, D. (2020). *The turnaway study: Ten years, a thousand women, and the consequences of having-or being denied-an abortion.* New York, NY: ANSIRH Press.

Griffin, G., O'Connor, O., Smyth, A., & O'Connor, A. (2019). *It's a yes! How Together for Yes repealed the Eight and transformed Irish society.* Dublin: Orpen Press.

Hadley, J. (1997). The "awfulisation" of abortion. *Choices, 26*(1), 7–8.

Irish Times. (2018). Safe, legal and rare: Full text of Taoiseach's abortion speech. *Irish Times.* Available at https://www.irishtimes.com/news/social-affairs/safe-legal-and-rare-full-text-of-taoiseach-s-abortion-speech-1.3373468 (accessed 9 June 2019).

Katz, J., & Tirone, V. (2015). From the agency line to the picket line: Neoliberal ideals, sexual realities, and arguments about abortion in the US. *Sex Roles, 73*(8), 311–318.

Kelly, K. (2014). The spread of "post abortion syndrome" as social diagnosis. *Social Science & Medicine, 102,* 18–25.

Kimport, K. (2012). (Mis)understanding abortion regret. *Symbolic Interaction, 35*(2), 105–122.

Kumar, A. (2013). Everything is not abortion stigma. *Women's Health Issues, 23*(6), 329–331.

Kumar, A., Hessini, L., & Mitchell, E. M. H. (2009). Conceptualising abortion stigma. *Culture, Health and Sexuality, 11*(6), 625–639.

Lee, E. (2003). *Abortion, motherhood and mental health.* New York, NY: Aldine de Gruyter.

Lee, E. (2017). Constructing abortion as a social problem: Sex selection and the British abortion debate. *Feminism and Psychology, 27*(2), 15–33.

Lowe, P. (2016). *Reproductive health and maternal sacrifice: Women, choice and responsibility.* London: Palgrave Macmillan.

Lowe, P., & Page, S. J. (2018). "On the wet side of the womb": The construction of mothers in anti-abortion activism in England and Wales. *European Journal of Women's Studies, 26*(2), 165–180.

Ludlow, J. (2012). Love and goodness: Toward a new abortion politics. *Feminist Studies, 38*(2), 474–483.

Lupton, D. (2013). *The social worlds of the unborn.* London: Palgrave Macmillan.

Major, B., Appelbaum, M., Beckman, L., Dutton, M. A., Russo, N. F., & West, C. (2009). Abortion and mental health: Evaluating the evidence. *American Psychologist, 64*(9), 863–890.

Martin, L. A., Hassinger, J. A., Debbink, M., & Harris, L. H. (2017). Dangertalk: Voices of abortion providers. *Social Science & Medicine, 18*(4), 75–83.

McDonnell, K. (1984). *Not an easy choice: Re-examining abortion.* London: South End Press.

McGreevy, R. (2018). The Citizens Assembly—A canny move on the road to repeal. *Irish Times*. Available at https://www.irishtimes.com/news/ireland/irish-news/the-citizens-assembly-a-canny-move-on-the-road-to-repeal-1.351 0373 (accessed 29 May 2020).

Millar, E. (2016). Mourned choices and grievable lives: The anti-abortion movement's influence in defining the abortion experience in Australia since the 1960s. *Gender & History, 28*(2), 501–519.

Millar, E. (2017). *Happy abortions: Our bodies in the era of choice*. London: Zed Books.

Petchesky, R. (1987). Fetal images: The power of visual culture in the politics of reproduction. *Feminist Studies, 13*(1), 263–292.

Pollitt, K. (2014). *Pro: Reclaiming abortion rights*. New York, NY: Picador.

Reinharz, S., & Davidman, L. (1992). *Feminist methods in social research*. New York, NY: Oxford University Press.

Rocca, C., Kimport, K., Roberts, S. C. M., Gould, H., Neuhaus, J., & Foster, D. G. (2015). Decision rightness and emotional responses to abortion in the United States: A longitudinal study. *PLOS ONE, 10*(7), e0128832.

RTE. (2018). RTE exit poll on eighth amendment projects: Yes 69.4% no 30.4%. Available at https://www.rte.ie/news/2018/0525/965899-eighth-amendment/ (accessd on 12 May 2020).

Sanger, C. (2017). *About abortion: Terminating pregnancy in 21-st century America*. New York, NY: Harvard University Press.

Silverman, D. (2001). *Interpreting qualitative data: Methods for analysing talk, text and interaction*. New York, NY: Thousand Oaks.

Sisson, G., & Kimport, K. (2014). Telling stories about abortion: Abortion-related plots in American film and television, 1916–2013. *Contraception, 89*(5), 413–418.

Solinger, R. (2013). *Reproductive politics: What everyone needs to know*. New York, NY: Oxford University Press.

Thomsen, C. (2013). From refusing stigmatization toward celebration: New directions for reproductive justice activism. *Feminist Studies, 39*(1), 149–158.

Weitz, T. A. (2010). Rethinking the mantra that abortion should be 'safe, legal, and rare'. *Journal of Women's History, 22*(3), 161–172.

CHAPTER 5

Conclusion

Abstract This chapter considers the criticisms levelled at the Together For Yes campaign and the legislation that followed the Repeal victory encoded in the Health Act (2018). It argues that had Together For Yes canvassed on a more radical platform then arguably some of the short-comings of the ensuing legislation may not have come to pass. The chapter then goes on to consider the post-Repeal abortion landscape in the Republic of Ireland, arguing that the best way to guarantee women's reproductive rights into the future is to defend against anti-abortion groups winning discursive ground in any future 'abortion debate'. It shows how such groups have successfully eroded abortion access in countries that once enjoyed more widespread abortion provision. One way of defending against this in the Republic of Ireland is to foster a culture of outspokenness around abortion that makes the case for abortion as a moral and social good.

Keywords Together For Yes · Health Act (2018) · Aontú · Anti-abortion politics

INTRODUCTION

I can testify that the party atmosphere in Dublin city in the hours following the Repeal result continued on in the days after. Alongside canvassers, fundraisers, volunteers and others both young and old, a

© The Author(s) 2020   91
D. Ralph, *Abortion and Ireland*,
https://doi.org/10.1007/978-3-030-58692-8_5

cross-generation of Repeal supporters revelled in the euphoria of their sometimes bruising and long-fought victory. On the streets, in café and bars, people seemed to be talking excitedly about little beyond the surprising and extraordinary referendum outcome. The iconic Repeal jumpers that many had worn for months in advance of voting day were still worn by people as a proud gesture of solidarity for weeks, even months, after polling day. And the overwhelming mandate for change to the status quo on Ireland's abortion laws received extensive and for the most part favourable coverage for several days in the international media and, in some cases, for several weeks in the Irish media (Calkin and Browne 2020; Conneely 2020).

A short distance from Dublin city centre, in the genteel suburb of Portobello, the atmosphere after the announcement of the result was somewhat different. Here, the general mood among many was more muted; people were somewhat solemn even if they were joyous too. Because here, on a wall beside a popular pub called The George Bernard Shaw, a mural had appeared the day before the vote bearing the smiling face of Savita Halappanavar. In the days following, thousands of people visited this mural (Ní Aodha 2018). The site around it became a sort of shrine to the young Indian dentist whose needless death acted as a catalyst in igniting a latent pro-choice movement to agitate for the removal of the Eighth (Specia 2018). Visitors lit candles on the pavement beneath the painting, bouquets of flowers piled up high by the wall. Hundreds of post-it notes, too, were affixed to the mural with handwritten messages. Some of these messages spoke of sadness and anger at the fate that befell the woman depicted on the wall. Others were of hope and gratitude now that the country had finally set in motion a process of reform around its restrictive abortion legislation. In fact, so busy was the footfall by the road outside The George Bernard Shaw that there were reports of traffic jams at that end of town (Neville 2018).

Savita Halappanavar's father, Andanappa Yalagi, spoke with the media the day of the referendum result (Specia 2018). He said he was happy that his daughter, at last, had received justice for what happened to her. He said that his family was grateful to the people of Ireland for not forgetting her, and he added that his family had one final request. The request was that the government name the abortion legislation to follow the referendum 'Savita's Law'. A number of government spokespersons and ministers said at the time that they would seriously consider the request, that it would be an apt name for the new legislation (Holland 2018).

This chapter considers what happened in the wake of the referendum, detailing the abortion legislation that was implemented on foot of the Repeal result. It offers a critique of certain aspects of that legislation that some felt went nowhere near far enough in providing reproductive freedom for women. It also offers a critique of Together For Yes, highlighting shortcomings in the organisers' campaigning strategies and suggesting a more critical reading of some of their pro-choice advocacy.

CONTINUITY AND CHANGE IN THE PRE- AND POST-REPEAL REPUBLIC OF IRELAND

As it turned out, the new legislation was not named Savita's Law. It was given the much more sombre and officious title Health (Regulation of Termination of Pregnancy) Act 2018 (or the Health Act 2018 for short). Nor did the festive mood generated in the immediate aftermath of the Yes side's win last long either. Instead, a lot of the exhilaration soon soured when details of the new legislation began to emerge, with this turning to outright disappointment among many by the time the final legislation was introduced on 1 January 2019. The Health Act 2018 meant that lawful terminations up to twelve weeks of pregnancy could be provided on request in Irish hospitals and clinics. Beyond this, abortion remains illegal and subject to criminal prosecution in the Republic of Ireland (Health Act 2018).

Several activist organisations—including the ARC—were deeply unhappy with the new legal regime around abortion provision codified in the Health Act 2018 (Bardon 2018). One of their prime complaints was the mandatory three-day waiting period, which forces women to wait 72 hours after an initial consultation with a doctor before an abortion can be carried out. This stipulation has no basis in medical best practice, and exists as an additional barrier to abortion access (Joyce et al. 2009). A second major complaint was the provision to allow medical practitioners to conscientiously abstain from participating in the provision of abortion services. This creates a further barrier to those who, in particular, may live in remote geographical areas with few alternative medical centres they can access (Side 2020).

Critics argue that both measures simply exist to generate a certain level of stigma and shame around the procedure (Enright et al. 2018; Fletcher 2018). The first infantilizes women by suggesting they go home and 'cool off' for a few days after making a decision to terminate an unwanted or unviable pregnancy. This can lead to what Sanger (2017) calls 'dignitary harm', as women are oftentimes subjected to invasive and humiliating questioning by medics during these screening consultations. Meanwhile, the second issue of conscientious objection creates a scenario whereby a medical professional can openly sit in judgement of the reproductive choices of a woman by outright refusing to provide medical assistance. This too can obviously lead to issues of dignitary harm.

From a legal perspective, de Londras (2020) has cautioned against the celebratory and uncritical accent placed on much of the Repeal discussion. She argues instead for a far more critical reading of the legislative framework that followed the referendum result. Repeal, she suggests, presented a once-in-a-generation opportunity for the legislature to create a new constitutional terrain where pregnant women would at last be recognised as bearers of reproductive freedom and bodily integrity (de Londras 2020). This opportunity, however, was squandered, as Irish lawmakers failed to break decisively with the pre-Repeal past. Certainly there has been significant liberalisation around abortion provision in the state with the passing of the Health Act 2018 through both houses of the parliament. Nevertheless, at the same time, there is also significant continuity between the pre- and post-Repeal legal landscapes, de Londras (2020) shows. Rather than foregrounding women's reproductive agency and decisional autonomy, what dominated politicians' discussions in drafting the Health Act 2018 were issues of how to manage the 'problem' of uncontrolled access to internet-bought abortion medications being taken without proper medical supervision and the tragedies facing couples receiving a diagnosis of a fatal foetal anomaly for their 'much wanted pregnancies' (de Londras 2020, 33). In this, the design of the new abortion regime is not only deeply patriarchal but also one that remains committed to 'natalist repronormativity' and continues to be more 'foetocentric' than woman-centric (de Londras 2020, 35). It also leaves intact the enormous power invested in medical professionals to control the reproductive lives of women and to act as both practical and moral gatekeepers to abortion access. Where, de Londras (2020) and others rightly wonder (see Enright et al. 2018; Fletcher 2018, 2020), are those voices vindicating a woman's right to privacy, a woman's right to bodily integrity, and finally a woman's right to choose?

Enright (2018) strikes a similarly critical note of the Health Act 2018. She argues that the post-Repeal legal emphasis on compassion for women is without question a welcome departure from the cruelties of the near-total abortion ban imposed by the Eighth Amendment. Nonetheless, the new legislation is some distance off the original ambitions of the Repeal movement for abortion law reform, Enright (2018) shows. The law demanded by grassroots Repeal activists would have framed women as independent political agents in possession of full reproductive autonomy and abortion as an unconditional entitlement of abortion-seeking women on a 'free, safe, legal' basis (Enright 2018). In the event, the eventual law delivered by the Minister for Health Simon Harris went on to frame abortion as something conditionally handed down by a newly compassionate but deeply patronising state only to those women it deems sufficiently vulnerable and in desperate enough need of its benevolent intervention (Enright 2018; Enright et al. 2018). This gap between the law demanded and the law delivered—or what might be considered the slippage between the clamour on the streets for abortion rights to the compromises of legislators' chambers—remains a source of profound frustration for many pro-choice activists (Calkin and Browne 2020). Weary though many are after the long campaign to repeal the Eighth, it is a gap they hope to bridge in future by regrouping to lobby elected representatives for better abortion legislation.

But the dissatisfaction among certain quarters of the pro-choice movement was not only with government for what they saw as the shortcomings of the Health Act 2018. Among some, there was a major unease too throughout much of the campaign with the messaging emerging from Together For Yes itself. Pro-choice critics of Together For Yes claim that the umbrella organisation's communication strategy went too far in trying to placate the supposedly anti-choice instincts of a naturally conservative constituency pundits often term 'middle Ireland' or Ireland's 'middle ground' (Duffy 2019; Enright 2019; McDonald et al. 2020; Redmond 2018). To appeal to this centrist constituency's instincts, Together For Yes had to suppress or redact the messier, more diverse voices of those also demanding repeal of the Eighth and whose voices also contributed to the grassroots' movement for abortion law reform. In real terms, this meant that Together For Yes deliberately silenced the voices of women of colour, of trans women, of trans men, of Traveller women, of women with intellectual and physical disabilities, of many working-class women, of sex worker women, and of several other minority women (Burns 2018; Campbell 2018; Rivetti 2019). If these women's experiences were given a platform, the implication is, then Together For Yes might have been viewed as 'extreme', as 'shrill', it might have been 'damaging to the campaign' and support from this target demographic of 'middle Ireland' might have haemorrhaged (Enright 2018).

A popular slogan deployed by Together For Yes during the campaign was 'Stand In Awe of All *Mná*' (Griffin et al. 2019). The word *mná* is the Gaelic plural of woman. However, as one disgruntled pro-choice advocate put it, Together For Yes ran an exceptionally respectable campaign dominated largely by women who were highly articulate, who were highly educated, and who would be viewed as highly 'white' (Burns 2018). Looking back, it is fair to say that on the campaign trail Together For Yes put forth very few black faces, very few brown faces, and the voices heard at its public demonstrations almost always had recognisably middle-class accents. Those from minority backgrounds were largely excluded from their high-profile events and denied spokesperson roles when engaging with the media, the opposition, or the political establishment. For the duration of the campaign, many pro-choice advocates made the practical decision to discipline themselves to the strict messaging strategy adopted by Together For Yes (Enright 2018). They held their tongues in the effort to secure passage of the referendum. Others, however, felt this was a sacrifice too far. They felt Together For Yes was betrayal of the more radical, inclusive and intersectional origins of the Repeal movement (Rivetti 2019). At the risk of sounding churlish, it could be suggested that a more accurate slogan for the Together For Yes campaign in place of 'Stand In Awe of All *Mná*' might have been 'Stand In Awe of Some *Mná*'.

ANTI-ABORTION BACKLASH

Arguably if a less restrictive social climate to speak about abortion 'loudly' had been available in Ireland in the lead-up to the referendum then the legal framework that followed the result would have come closer to realising the more radical aims of the Repeal movement. If this had been available, perhaps too Together For Yes might have taken a more inclusive approach to its campaign. However, it is possible that in the aftermath of Repeal the framing discourses and social meanings of abortion in the country will expand and move away from the 'hushed tones' of old. In fact, given the scale of the Repeal victory it could be expected that they will. A generation of pro-choice advocates have been galvanised by the Repeal success, and they are unlikely to easily give up any gains they have made around abortion access and reproductive rights (Calkin and Browne 2020).

That said, at the same time the tenacity of anti-abortion groups is nothing if not remarkable (Browne and Nash 2020). Even when their views seem to be out of sync with mainstream public opinion they keep fighting what in their eyes is the good fight (Beckman 2017). Anti-abortion advocates are well-organised, remarkably even if opaquely well-funded, and it is conceivable that, in the case of Ireland, such groups could successfully lobby politicians, legislators and others at some point in the future to alter again the country's abortion regime in a more restrictive direction. In fact, as I show below, a highly coordinated backlash is already underway against Irish women with precisely such ambitions driving it.

Prior to the repealing of the Eighth abortion opponents in Ireland have long imported in an almost copy-paste manner the anti-abortion tactics familiar from the American anti-abortion playbook (Earner-Byrne and Urquhart 2019.) And now that abortion has been legalised in Ireland, a number of these American-style anti-abortion strategies have been already in evidence. For instance, as are often found in the United States, several Crisis Pregnancy Centres (CPCs) providing sometimes misleading information on women's reproductive choices and attempting to dissuade them from abortion have opened up since 1 January 2019 (Hogan 2019). These CPCs have been exposed in setting up spurious websites that mimic most design features of the official Health Service Executive's abortion information websites with the intention of luring abortion-seeking women through their doors. Another tactic long familiar from the American 'abortion wars', anti-abortionists in the Republic of Ireland have been harassing women on their way into Ireland's newly opened abortion care clinics, attempting to provide them with last-minute 'pavement counselling' to prevent a procedure going ahead (Moore 2019). This 'pavement counselling' often involves threats of physical violence and verbal abuse of women who have made the decision to no longer be pregnant. The government has promised to introduce a law putting in place 'exclusion zones' around clinics and GP surgeries proving abortion care. But this legislation is yet to pass. And it is not only abortion-seeking women this harassment has been directed at. Doctors who have signed up to provide termination of pregnancy services have been at the receiving end of this campaign of intimidation too (Hogan 2019).

It is fair to say that anti-choice politicians did not quite take the referendum result lying down either (Abortion Rights Campaign 2019). No sooner had the count been read out and their focus shifted to efforts to frustrate and dilute progress of pro-Repeal laws through the legislature (Enright 2019). In both the upper and lower houses of the parliament, anti-choice TDs and senators made long rambling speeches on the various aspects of the proposed new legislation to accusations that they were filibustering (Power 2018). Nonetheless, they pressed doggedly ahead with several amendments that had no numerical chance of being passed in either chamber. One of the most controversial of these amendments included the proposal that viewing ultrasound imaging of a pregnancy and listening to the foetal heartbeat recording become mandatory for all abortion-seeking women (Finn 2018). Another was that funerary services of foetal remains through either burial or cremation become a legal requirement for all women following a termination subject to penalties and fines for non-compliance (Finn 2018). All anti-choice politicians' amendments were defeated at the early stages of the legislative process.

Yet it seems that these various setbacks and defeats have not deterred many in the Irish anti-choice movement from their objectives. In fact, for some it has presented a political opportunity to represent what they see as the now-disenfranchised voice of the 33 per cent of the electorate who voted to retain the Eighth (Kelly 2018). To this end, an explicitly pro-life political party called *Aontú* has formed seeking to capture the votes of this potentially sizable pro-life constituency. *Aontú*, which means unity in Irish, formed in the immediate aftermath of the Repeal referendum with the express intention of protecting the life of what it terms 'preborn humans', whose rights, the party claims, have been 'shockingly stripped of legislative protection' since the removal of the Eighth Amendment (cited in Leahy 2019, para. 4). *Aontú* fielded candidates in the local elections in December 2019 and won three seats in the town and city councils. Meanwhile, in February 2020 during the general election it won a single seat in the national parliament. Given how recently the party was established, *Aontú* spokespersons said they were happy with the results and that they will continue their work to roll back on the reproductive healthcare options now afforded women under the Health Act 2018. It is not realistic that *Aontú* will be any major political force in Irish politics in the coming years. However, what is realistic is that *Aontú* continues to grow its grassroots support and membership base and that in future elections the party wins not one but two or three or four seats in the national parliament. Considering that government formation in Ireland routinely involves the dominant parties forming coalitions with smaller parties to achieve a working majority, it is perfectly conceivable in such a scenario that *Aontú* might find itself in the enviable position of 'king-maker' for a potential future government. One concession almost certain to be demanded by *Aontú* in a case like this would be a row back on some recent pro-choice gains made in the legislative arena.

BEYOND REPEAL

What is clear from abortion politics in other parts of the world is that reproductive rights regimes do not remain static. Like other laws, they are not covenants. They are laws that are made by lawmakers, and as such are subject to change. And that change may not always be in a positive direction from the perspective of pro-choice advocates. As the Repeal campaign began to mobilise in Ireland following the death of Savita Halappanavar in 2012, around this same time a counter-mobilisation of sorts was taking place in other, nearby European countries which once enjoyed relatively liberal abortion regimes (Council of Europe 2017). For instance, in Spain in 2014 the then-government tabled a proposal to limit abortion to cases of rape only, but ultimately failed in winning sufficient support for this measure (Council of Europe 2017). In 2016 the Polish government put a similar bill before parliament that would have criminalised abortion in almost all circumstances, only voting down the bill after a massive public outcry against it (Council of Europe 2017). Meanwhile, in Slovakia this past year major protests by anti-abortion campaigners have called on the government there to pass legislation to severely row back on current laws, which permit abortion up to twelve weeks (Reuters 2019).

But perhaps the present situation in the United States offers the most cautionary tale for those who want major legal barriers to abortion access to remain a feature of Ireland's past. Abortion may be technically and constitutionally legal still in the United States. Yet so drastically has the legislative framework around the procedure been winnowed away in recent years that the legally sanctioned grounds for obtaining a pregnancy termination have all but disappeared in several states now (Guttmacher Institute 2016). Since the administration of President Donald Trump took control in 2016, they have enthusiastically overseen a proliferation of restrictive measures around abortion (Guttmacher Institute 2019).

This has involved starving abortion providers of state and federal-level funding, eliminating the requirement to provide non-directive pregnancy counselling, and making abortion referral exceedingly difficult to justify going by precise letter of the law (Guttmacher Institute 2019). All of this has ultimately contributed to hundreds of clinics closing, particularly in conservative heartlands where such amendments have met with little resistance. Overhauling the country's abortion laws was one of the core policy promises on which Trump was elected to office. And in January 2020, in an effort to shore up his pro-life credentials for his re-election campaign, Trump was the first sitting United States president to attend the annual March For Life rally in Washington DC (BBC 2020). The March For Life rally was started in 1974, in the immediate wake of the 1973 Roe v Wade ruling.

So how might pro-choicers protect against such an eventuality ever occurring in the Republic of Ireland? How, in other words, might they prevent what has been happening to Roe v Wade happening to Repeal?

One way of ensuring against this is for pro-choice voices to remain audible in the public discourse on abortion. What remains rare in much public discourse are accounts of abortion that present the procedure not only as a normal part of women's reproductive lives and health care but as a positive social and moral good for women specifically and society more generally. Such an abortion narrative needs to be articulated much more loudly, much more vehemently, much more consistently. Where women remain silent about their abortions—as well as the silence of all the boyfriends, husbands, partners, family members, friends, work colleagues, medical practitioners and others who helped abortion-seeking women organise it—those hostile to abortion rights are adept at filling the vacuum (Pollitt 2014). And into this vacuum, as has been witnessed in numerous other contexts, they routinely circulate dubiously founded claims about the injurious nature of the procedure, 'proving' that women suffer irreversible trauma, regret and loss post-abortion (Rocca et al. 2015).

In fact, and more precisely, what is called for is the development of a culture of outspokenness on a subject where, even among those who are in favour of liberal abortion provision, people have traditionally stayed quiet. The reproductive rights women in Ireland have at last gained over their bodies have been hard-won. For these rights to remain intact—for them to remain won, so to speak—it is vital that a shift in advocacy occurs, to paraphrase Arveda Kissling (2018) again, away from that of a tamed 'whisper' to a more resoundingly articulated 'shout'. This would ensure that framing discourses seeking to stigmatise abortion, abortion providers, as well as anyone associated with the procedure are met with strong counter-framing discourses striving to normalise and destigmatise it (Millar 2020).

This crucial work of counter-framing, however, cannot be left any longer to pro-choice women alone. It is both unfair and unrealistic to call on those with a history of abortion experience to continually share in publicly consumable narratives the most intimate details of their private lives in an effort to keep anti-abortion forces at bay. Unsurprisingly, once the Repeal referendum was over and once the result was in, the publicly shared abortion stories from women stopped. To have to repeat this kind of emotional storytelling labour over and over would be exhausting. A key factor, then, in the development of any future culture of outspokenness on abortion is that the discursive work of normalising the procedure needs to be shouldered by all those supportive of women's rights to reproductive autonomy and against all forms of reproductive coercion. In the run-up to the Repeal vote, Mara Clarke of the Abortion Support Network made the telling remark that, 'It takes a village to have an abortion' (Clarke, cited in Campbell 2018, para. 14). By this she meant that when you include all the professionals, para-professionals, friends, family, partners, lovers, ex-lovers, childcarers, work colleagues, acquaintances and others who are directly or indirectly involved in a women ending a pregnancy, then there must be many, many people in communities everywhere who have had some meaningful interaction with the issue of abortion. A culture of outspokenness begins, then, when not just the women themselves with abortion histories become vocal about those experiences but when all those others start to speak up too.

In practical terms, this would involve having far more pro-choice men speak out in favour of abortion provision. It would involve those in the media being more proactively pro-choice in their broadcasts, in their programming, in their editorials. It would involve those working in all areas of the culture industry—including music, film, literature, television—representing pregnancy termination in less dramatic ways and instead depicting abortion in a manner that resists the usual tired tropes and stereotypes associated with it. It would involve politicians, too, taking up firm pro-choice positions not only when it happens to be politically expedient and popular to do so but also at times when it may be in fact unfashionable and unpopular to do just this. This is the true measure of political bravery and leadership.

If such actions were to take root, abortion could potentially move away from the arena of taboo, transgression and the non-normative it has long occupied in the minds of many. If such actions were to be normalised, then in time the routine gynaecological procedure that abortion is for most women who have experienced it might begin to be understood as just that. If such actions were to be embedded in the culture, abortion-seeking women might cease be viewed in any residual sense as penitents and sinners but simply as patients and citizens.

Indeed, if such actions were to become routine, a day might soon arrive when abortion story-sharing by women ceases to be a political necessity in the effort to secure their reproductive rights and bodily integrity. And such a day, when women like those behind #Twowomentravel are no longer called upon to turn their private crises into public protests, is surely a day to be welcomed.

REFERENCES

Abortion Rights Campaign. (2019). *Why Ireland still needs ARC and why ARC still needs you!* Abortion Rights Campaign. Available at https://www.abortionrightscampaign.ie/2019/05/12/why-ireland-still-needs-arc-and-why-arc-still-needs-you/ (accessed 25 May 2020).

Arveda Kissling, E. (2018). *From a whisper to a shout: Abortion activism and social media.* London: Repeater Books.

Bardon, S. (2018). Abolish three-day waiting period for abortion, TD demands. *Irish Times.* Available at https://www.irishtimes.com/news/politics/abolish-three-day-waiting-period-for-abortion-td-demands-1.3540373 (accessed 9 July 2019).

BBC. (2020). *Trump first president to attend anti-abortion rally.* BBC. Available at https://www.bbc.com/news/world-us-canada-51239795 (accessed 31 May 2020).

Beckman, L. J. (2017). Abortion in the United States: The continuing controversy. *Feminism & Psychology, 27*(1), 101–113.

Browne, K., & Nash, C. J. (2020). Losing Ireland: Heteroactivist responses to the 8th Amendment in Canada and the UK. In K. Browne & S. Calkin (Eds.), *After repeal: Rethinking abortion politics* (pp. 207–223). London: Zed Books.

Burns, E. (2018). *Intersectionality and the Irish abortion rights campaign of 2018.* Available at https://emmaqburns.com/2018/09/19/10thdss-int

ersectionality-and-the-irish-abortion-rights-campaign-of-2018/ (accessed 28 May 2020).

Calkin, S., & Browne, K. (2020). Introduction. In K. Browne & S. Calkin (Eds.), *After repeal: Rethinking abortion politics* (pp. 1–19). London: Zed Books.

Campbell, E. (2018). My experience of the Together For Yes campaign. *Sexual Reproductive Health Matters*. Available at http://www.srhm.org/news/my-experience-of-the-together-for-yes-tfy-campaign/ (accessed 28 May 2020).

Conneely, A. (2020). Malta looks to Ireland in campaign for legal abortion. *RTE*. Available at https://www.rte.ie/news/world/2020/0525/1141515-abortion/ (accessed 28 May 2020).

Council of Europe. (2017). *Women's sexual and reproductive health and rights in Europe*. Brussels: Council of Europe.

de Londras, F. (2020). "A hope raised and then defeated"? The continuing harms of Irish abortion law. *Feminist Review, 124*, 33–50.

Duffy, S. (2019). *A change is gonna come: Reflections on the repeal campaign.* Sandra Duffy. Available at https://sandraduffy.wordpress.com/2019/01/07/a-change-is-gonna-come-reflections-on-the-repeal-campaign/ (accessed 28 May 2020).

Earner-Byrne, L., & Urquhart, D. (2019). *The Irish abortion journey, 1920–2018*. London: Palgrave.

Enright, A. (2018). Personal stories are precious things and they made the difference. *Irish Times*. Available at https://www.irishtimes.com/opinion/anne-enright-personal-stories-are-precious-things-and-they-made-the-differ ence-1.3510189 (accessed 28 May 2020).

Enright, M. (2019). Abortion law in Ireland: Reflecting on reform. In L. Black & P. Dunne (Eds.), *Law and gender in modern Ireland: Critique and reform* (pp. 73–89). Oxford: Hart Publishing.

Enright, M., Fletcher, R., de Londras, F., & Conway, V. (2018). *Position paper on the updated general scheme of the Health (Regulation of Termination of Pregnancy) Bill 2018*. Lawyers for Choice. Available at https://lawyers4choice.files.wordpress.com/2018/08/position-paper-1.pdf (accessed 28 May 2020).

Finn, C. (2018). Nine TDs want law to ensure aborted foetuses are buried or cremated. *The Journal*. Available at https://www.thejournal.ie/abortion-law-burial-foetus-4319054-Nov2018/ (accessed 28 May 2020).

Fletcher, R. (2018). #RepealingThe8th: Translating travesty, global conversation, and the Irish abortion referendum. *Feminist Legal Studies, 26*(3), 233–259.

Fletcher, R. (2020). Cheeky witnessing. *Feminist Review, 124*, 24–141.

Griffin, G., O'Connor, O., Smyth, A., & O'Connor, A. (2019). *It's a yes! How Together For Yes repealed the Eight and transformed Irish society*. Dublin: Orpen Press.

Guttmacher Institute. (2016). *Fact sheet: Abortion in the United States.* Available at https://www.guttmacher.org/sites/default/files/factsheet/fb_induced_abortion_3.pdf (accessed 22 Nov 2019).

Guttmacher Institute. (2019). *What the Trump administration's final regulatory changes mean for Title X.* Guttmacher Institute. Available at https://www.guttmacher.org/article/2019/03/what-trump-admini strations-final-regulatory-changes-mean-title-x (accessed 31 May 2020).

Health Act. (2018). *Health (Regulation of Termination of Pregnancy) Act 2018.* Dublin: Oireachtas.

Hogan, C. (2019). Why Ireland's battle over abortion is far from over. *Guardian.* Available at https://www.theguardian.com/lifeandstyle/2019/oct/03/why-irelands-battle-over-abortion-is-far-from-over-anti-abortionists (accessed 21 Nov 2019).

Holland, K. (2018). Savita Halappanavar's parents "really, really happy" after abortion vote. *Irish Times.* Available at https://www.irishtimes.com/news/social-affairs/savita-halappanavar-s-parents-really-really-happy-after-abortion-vote-1.3509839 (accessed 28 May 2020).

Joyce, T. J., Henshaw, S. K., Dennis, A., Finer, L. B., & Blanchard, K. (2009). *The impact of state mandatory counseling and waiting period laws on abortion: A literature review.* New York: Guttmacher Institute.

Kelly, F. (2018). Peadar Tóibín suspended from Sinn Féin over abortion law vote. *Irish Times.* Available at https://www.irishtimes.com/news/politics/peadar-t%C3%B3ib%C3%ADn-suspended-from-sinn-f%C3%A9in-over-abortion-law-vote-1.3682771.html (accessed 28 May 2020).

Leahy, P. (2019). Aontú making a place for itself in Irish politics, says Toibin. *Irish Times.* Available at https://www.irishtimes.com/news/politics/aont%C3%BA-making-a-place-for-itself-in-irish-politics-says-t%C3%B3ib%C3%ADn-1.3894746 (accessed 21 Nov 2019).

McDonald, N., Antosik-Parsons, K., Till, K. E., Callan, J., & Kearns, G. (2020). Campaigning for choice: Canvassing as feminist pedagogy in Dublin Bay North. In K. Browne & S. Calkin (Eds.), *After repeal: Rethinking abortion politics* (pp. 124–144). London: Zed Books.

Millar, E. (2020). Abortion stigma as a social process. *Women's Studies International Forum, 78*(2), 1023–1028.

Moore, A. (2019). Minister backs exclusion zones as US anti-abortion groups target Ireland. *Irish Independent.* Available at https://www.independent.ie/breaking-news/irish-news/minister-backs-exclusion-zones-as-us-antiabortion-groups-target-ireland-37826853.html (accessed 21 Nov 2019).

Neville, S. (2018). People have been leaving flowers and notes at the Savita mural in Dublin. *Irish Examiner.* Available at https://www.irishexaminer.com/breakingnews/discover/people-have-been-leaving-flowers-and-notes-at-the-savita-mural-in-dublin-845251.html (accessed 28 May 2020).

Ní Aodha, G. (2018). Savita mural artist: "I've been painting a long time, I've never seen a reaction like that before". *The Journal.* https://www.thejournal.ie/savita-mural-artist-4044389-May2018/ (accessed 28 May 2020).

Pollitt, K. (2014). *Pro: Reclaiming abortion rights.* New York: Picador.

Power, J. (2018). Bishops "dismayed" at voices of abortion opponents being ignored. *Irish Times.* Available at https://www.irishtimes.com/news/politics/bishops-dismayed-at-voices-of-abortion-opponents-being-ignored-1.3722429.html (accessed 28 May 2020).

Redmond, S. (2018). *It's been two months now.* Feminist Ire. Available at https://feministire.com/2018/07/27/its-been-two-months-now/ (accessed 28 May 2020).

Reuters. (2019). *Tens of thousands march for ban on abortion in Slovakia.* Reuters.com. Available at https://www.reuters.com/article/us-slovakia-abortion/tens-of-thousands-march-for-ban-on-abortions-in-slovakia-idUSKBN1W70I5 (accessed 22 Nov 2019).

Rivetti, P. (2019). Race, identity, and the state after the Irish abortion referendum. *Feminist Review, 122,* 121–188.

Rocca, C., Kimport, K., Roberts, S. C. M., Gould, H., Neuhaus, J., & Foster, D. G. (2015). Decision rightness and emotional responses to abortion in the United States: A longitudinal study. *PLoS ONE, 10*(7), e0128832.

Sanger, C. (2017). *About abortion: Terminating pregnancy in 21-st century America.* New York: Harvard University Press.

Side, K. (2020). Abortion im/mobility: Spatial consequences in the Republic of Ireland. *Feminist Review, 124,* 15–31.

Specia, M. (2018). How Savita Halappanavar's death spurred Ireland's abortion rights campaign. *New York Times.* Available at https://www.nytimes.com/2018/05/27/world/europe/savita-halappanavar-ireland-abortion.html (accessed 12 June 2019).

References

Abortion Rights Campaign. (2016). *Submission to the citizens assembly.* Available at www.abortionrightscampaign.ie (accessed 1 June 2019).

Abortion Rights Campaign. (2017). *Time to speak out: 2017 Abortion Rights Campaign Speak Out.* Abortion Rights Campaign. Available at https://www.abortionrightscampaign.ie/event/time-to-speak-out-2017-abortion-rights-campaign-speak-out/ (accessed 28 May 2020).

Abortion Rights Campaign. (2019). *Why Ireland still needs ARC and why ARC still needs you!* Abortion Rights Campaign. Available at https://www.abortionrightscampaign.ie/2019/05/12/why-ireland-still-needs-arc-and-why-arc-still-needs-you/ (accessed 25 May 2020).

Allen, M. (2014). Narrative diversity and sympathetic abortion: What online storytelling reveals about the prescribed norms of the mainstream movements. *Symbolic Interaction, 38*(1), 42–63.

Allport, G. (1954). *The nature of prejudice.* Reading: Addison-Wesley.

Andeweg, A. (2017). Cultural dimensions of sexual liberalization. *Sexuality & Culture, 21*(2), 339–342.

Armstrong, K. (2019). Together for Yes former co-directors named in TIME 100 list. *Irish Independent.* Available at https://www.independent.ie/irish-news/news/together-for-yes-former-co-directors-named-in-time-100-list-38024917.html (accessed 28 May 2020).

Arnold, B. (2009). *The Irish Gulag: How the state betrayed its innocent children.* Dublin: Gill & Macmillan.

Arveda Kissling, E. (2018). *From a whisper to a shout: Abortion activism and social media.* London: Repeater Books.

Bacik, I. (2004). *Kicking and screaming: Dragging Ireland into the twenty-first century*. Dublin: O'Brien Press.

Bacik, I. (2015). Abortion and the law in Ireland. In A. Quilty, S. Kennedy, & C. Conlon (Eds.), *The abortion papers Ireland: Volume 2* (pp. 104–117). Cork: Cork University Press.

Baird, B. (1998). *"Somebody was going to disapprove anyway": Re-thinking histories of abortion in South Australia*. Ph.D. dissertation, Flinders University.

Baird, B., & Millar, E. (2019). More than stigma: Interrogating counter narratives of abortion. *Sexualities, 22*(7–8), 1110–1126.

Bardon, S. (2018). Abolish three-day waiting period for abortion, TD demands. *Irish Times*. Available at https://www.irishtimes.com/news/politics/abolish-three-day-waiting-period-for-abortion-td-demands-1.3540373 (accessed 9 July 2019).

Barry, U. (1988). Abortion in Ireland. *Feminist Review, 29*(2), 57–66.

BBC. (2016, August 22). *#TwoWomenTravel—Live-tweeting the journey for an abortion*. BBC. Available at https://www.bbc.com/news/blogs-trending-37156673 (accessed 26 May 2020).

BBC. (2020). *Trump first president to attend anti-abortion rally*. BBC. Available at https://www.bbc.com/news/world-us-canada-51239795 (accessed 31 May 2020).

Beatty, A. (2013). Irish modernity and the politics of contraception, 1979–1993. *New Hibernia Review, 17*(3), 100–118.

Beckman, L. J. (2017). Abortion in the United States: The continuing controversy. *Feminism & Psychology, 27*(1), 101–113.

Belfrage, M., Ortíz Ramírez, O., & Sorhaind, A. (2019). Story circles and abortion stigma in Mexico: A mixed-methods evaluation of a new intervention for reducing individual level abortion stigma. *Culture, Health and Sexuality, 1*, 96–111.

Beynon-Jones, S. M. (2017). Untroubling abortion: A discourse analysis of women's accounts. *Feminism & Psychology, 27*(2), 225–242.

Bloomer, F., & O'Dowd, K. (2014). Restricted access to abortion in the Republic of Ireland and Northern Ireland: Exploring abortion tourism and barrier to legal reform. *Culture, Health and Sexuality, 16*(4), 366–380.

Borland, E. (2014). Storytelling, identity, and strategy: Perceiving shifting obstacles in the fight for abortion rights in Argentina. *Sociological Perspectives, 57*(4), 488–505.

Browne, K., & Nash, C. J. (2020). Losing Ireland: Heteroactivist responses to the 8th Amendment in Canada and the UK. In K. Browne & S. Calkin (Eds.), *After repeal: Rethinking abortion politics* (pp. 207–223). London: Zed Books.

Burns, E. (2018). *Intersectionality and the Irish abortion rights campaign of 2018*. Available at https://emmaqburns.com/2018/09/19/10thdss-int

ersectionality-and-the-irish-abortion-rights-campaign-of-2018/ (accessed 28 May 2020).

Butler, J. (2016). The horrific court case involving a young pregnant brain-dead woman might not be a one-off. *The Journal*. Available at https://www.thejournal.ie/readme/eight-amendment-abortion-rights-2685815-Mar2016/ (accessed 28 May 2020).

Calkin, S. (2019a). Healthcare not airfare! Art, abortion and political agency in Ireland. *Gender, Place & Culture, 26*(3), 338–361.

Calkin, S. (2019b). Towards a political geography of abortion. *Political Geography, 69*(2), 22–29.

Calkin, S. (2020). Abortion pills in Ireland and beyond: What can the 8th Amendment referendum tell us about the future of self-managed abortion? In K. Browne & S. Calkin (Eds.), *After repeal: Rethinking abortion politics* (pp. 73–89). London: Zed Books.

Calkin, S., & Browne, K. (2020). Introduction. In K. Browne & S. Calkin (Eds.), *After repeal: Rethinking abortion politics* (pp. 1–19). London: Zed Books.

Cameron, S. (2010). Induced abortion and psychological sequelae. *Best Practice & Research Clinical Obstetrics & Gynaecology, 24*(5), 657–665.

Campbell, E. (2018). My experience of the Together for Yes campaign. *Sexual Reproductive Health Matters*. Available at http://www.srhm.org/news/my-experience-of-the-together-for-yes-tfy-campaign/ (accessed 28 May 2020).

Canavan, J. (2012). Family and family change in Ireland: An overview. *Journal of Family Issues, 33*(2), 10–28.

Cannold, L. (1998). *The abortion myth: Feminism, morality, and the hard choices women make*. New York: Wesleyan University Press.

Carolan, M. (2019). Family of pregnant woman kept on life support gets HSE apology. *Irish Times*. Available at https://www.irishtimes.com/news/crime-and-law/courts/high-court/family-of-pregnant-woman-kept-on-life-support-gets-hse-apology-1.4089935 (accessed 28 May 2020).

Citizens' Assembly. (2017). *First report and recommendations of the Citizens' Assembly: The Eighth Amendment of the Constitution*. Dublin: Citizens' Assembly.

Cockrill, K. (2014). Commentary: Imagine a world without abortion stigma. *Women & Health, 54*(7), 662–665.

Cockrill, K., & Biggs, A. (2018). Can stories reduce abortion stigma? Findings from a longitudinal cohort study. *Culture, Health & Sexuality, 20*(3), 335–350.

Cockrill, K., & Nack, A. (2013). "I'm not that type of person": Managing the stigma of having an abortion. *Deviant Behaviour, 34*(12), 973–990.

Condit, C. (1990). *Decoding abortion rhetoric: Communicating social change*. Chicago: University of Illinois Press.

Conneely, A. (2020). Malta looks to Ireland in campaign for legal abortion. *RTE*. Available at https://www.rte.ie/news/world/2020/0525/1141515-abortion/ (accessed 28 May 2020).

Connolly, L. (2002). *The Irish women's movement: From revolution to devolution*. New York: Palgrave.

Connor, D. (2018). Savita Halappanavar's parents call for Yes vote. *RTE*. Available at https://www.rte.ie/news/eighth-amendment/2018/0520/964749-savita-halappanavar/ (accessed 22 June 2018).

Constitution of Ireland. (1937). *Irish Constitution*. Dublin: Department of the Taoiseach.

Council of Europe. (2017). *Women's sexual and reproductive health and rights in Europe*. Brussels: Council of Europe.

Cowan, S. K. (2014). Secrets and misperceptions: The creation of self-fulfilling illusions. *Sociological Science, 1*(2), 466–492.

Cowan, S. K. (2017). Enacted abortion stigma in the United States. *Social Science & Medicine, 177*(4), 259–268.

Cox, C. (2009). Institutionalisation in Irish history and society. In M. McAuliffe, K. O'Donnell, & L. Lane (Eds.), *Palgrave advances in Irish history* (pp. 169–190). New York: Palgrave Macmillan.

Crowley, E. (2013). *Your place or mine? Community and belonging in 21st century Ireland*. Dublin: Orpen Press.

Crowley, U., & Kitchin, R. (2008). Producing "decent girls": Governmentality and the moral geographies of sexual conduct in Ireland. *Gender, Place and Culture: A Journal of Feminist Geography, 15*(4), 55–72.

Cullen, P. (2013). "Horrendous, barbaric, inhumane": Savita's husband gives his verdict. *Irish Times*. https://www.irishtimes.com/news/horrendous-barbaric-inhumane-savita-s-husband-gives-his-verdict-1.1367234 (accessed 28 May 2020).

Dadlez, E. M., & Andrews, W. L. (2010). Post-abortion syndrome: Creating an affliction. *Bioethics, 24*(9), 445–452.

Daly, M. (2006). Marriage, fertility and women's lives in twentieth-century Ireland (c.1900–c.1970). *Women's History Review, 15*(4), 571–585.

Daly, M. (2016). *Sixties Ireland: Reshaping the economy, state and society, 1957–1973*. Cambridge: Cambridge University Press.

Darcy, E. (2020). *In her shoes. Women of the Eight: A memoir and anthology*. Dublin: New Island Books.

de Londras, F. (2020). "A hope raised and then defeated"? The continuing harms of Irish abortion law. *Feminist Review, 124*, 33–50.

de Londras, F., & Enright, M. (2018). *Repealing the 8th: Reforming Irish abortion law*. Bristol: Policy Press.

de Londras, F., & Graham, L. (2013). Impossible floodgates and unworkable analogies in the Irish abortion debate. *Irish Journal of Legal Studies, 3*(3), 54–75.

De Zordo, S., Mishtal, J., & Anton, L. (2016). *A fragmented landscape: Abortion governance and protest logics in Europe*. New York: Berghahn Books.

Delay, C. (2018). Pills, potions, and purgatives: Women and abortion methods in Ireland, 1900–1950. *Women's History Review, 28*(3), 479–499.

Dickson-Swift, V., James, E. L., Kippen, S., & Liamputtong, P. (2007). Doing sensitive research: What challenges do qualitative researchers face? *Qualitative Research, 7*(3), 327–353.

Doyle, K. (2017). Simon Harris: I felt ashamed at abortion treatment and changed my view. *Irish Independent*. Available at https://www.independent.ie/irish-news/politics/simon-harris-i-felt-ashamed-at-abortion-treatment-and-changed-my-view-36443198.html (accessed 15 May 2019).

Duffy, S. (2019). *A change is gonna come: Reflections on the repeal campaign*. Sandra Duffy. Available at https://sandraduffy.wordpress.com/2019/01/07/a-change-is-gonna-come-reflections-on-the-repeal-campaign/ (accessed 28 May 2020).

Dully, H. (2017). *Balance, binary debate and missing women: A discourse analysis and creative response to 30 years of the abortion debate on RTÉ current affairs television, 1983–2013*. Ph.D. dissertation, NUI Galway.

Duncan, P., Glenza, J., & Rice-Oxley, M. (2019). US more anti-abortion than other developed countries—Global poll. *Guardian*. Available at https://www.theguardian.com/world/2019/may/17/us-more-anti-abortion-than-other-developed-countries-global-poll (accessed 21 Nov 2019).

Earner-Byrne, L. (2007). *Mother and child: Maternity and child welfare in Dublin, 1922–1960*. Manchester: Manchester University Press.

Earner-Byrne, L., & Urquhart, D. (2019). *The Irish abortion journey, 1920–2018*. London: Palgrave.

Enright, A. (2018a). Personal stories are precious things and they made the difference. *Irish Times*. Available at https://www.irishtimes.com/opinion/anne-enright-personal-stories-are-precious-things-and-they-made-the-difference-1.3510189 (accessed 28 May 2020).

Enright, M. (2018b). The enemy of the good: Reflections on Ireland's new abortion legislation. *feminists@law, 8*(2), 1–12.

Enright, M. (2019). Abortion law in Ireland: Reflecting on reform. In L. Black & P. Dunne (Eds.), *Law and gender in modern Ireland: Critique and reform* (pp. 73–89). Oxford: Hart Publishing.

Enright, M., & Cloatre, E. (2018). Transformative illegality: How condoms 'became legal' in Ireland, 1991–1993. *Feminist Legal Studies, 26*(3), 261–284.

Enright, M., Fletcher, R., de Londras, F., & Conway, V. (2018). *Position paper on the updated general scheme of the Health (Regulation of Termination of Pregnancy) Bill 2018*. Lawyers for Choice. Available at https://lawyers4choice. files.wordpress.com/2018/08/position-paper-1.pdf (accessed 28 May 2020).

Escoffier, J. (Ed.). (2003). *Sexual revolution*. New York: Thunder's Mouth Press.

Fahey, T., & Layte, R. (2007). Family and sexuality. In T. Fahey, H. Russell, & C. T. Whelan (Eds.), *Best of times? The social impact of the Celtic Tiger* (pp. 155–174). Dublin: Institute of Public Administration.

Farrell, E. (Ed.). (2012). *'She said she was in the family way': Pregnancy and infancy in modern Ireland*. London: The Institute of Historical Research.

Ferriter, D. (2009). *Occasions of sin: Sex and society in modern Ireland*. London: Profile Books.

Ferriter, D. (2014, August 23). The Irish abortion question has always been linked to class, secrecy and moral judgement. *Irish Times*. Available at https://www.irishtimes.com/news/social-affairs/the-irish-abortion-que stion-has-always-been-linked-to-class-secrecy-and-moral-judgment-1.1905362 (accessed 26 May 2020).

Fianna Fail. (2018). *Speech by Michael Martin on debate on report of Committee on 8th Amendment*. Fianna Fail. Available at https://www.fiannafail.ie/spe ech-by-micheal-martin-on-debate-on-report-of-committee-on-8th-amendm ent-18th-jan-2018/ (accessed 1 June 2019).

Filipovic, J. (2016). With Pro Katha Pollitt gives the abortion rights movement its modern credo. *Signs: Journal of Women in Culture and Society, 41*(4), 979–999.

Fine, G. A. (1995). Public narration and group culture: Discerning discourse in social movements. In H. Johnston & B. Klandermans (Eds.), *Social movements and culture* (pp. 127–143). New York: University of Minnesota Press.

Finn, C. (2018). Nine TDs want law to ensure aborted foetuses are buried or cremated. *The Journal*. Available at https://www.thejournal.ie/abortion-law-burial-foetus-4319054-Nov2018/ (accessed 28 May 2020).

Finnegan, F. (2004). *Do penance or perish: Magdalen Asylums in Ireland*. Oxford: Oxford University Press.

Fischer, C. (2016). Gender, nation, and the politics of shame: Magdalen laundries and the institutionalization of feminine transgression in modern Ireland. *Signs: Journal of Women in Culture and Society, 41*(4), 821–843.

Fischer, C. (2017). Revealing Ireland's "proper" heart: Apology, shame, nation. *Hypatia, 32*(4), 751–767.

Fischer, C. (2019). Abortion and reproduction in Ireland: Shame, nation-building and the affective politics of place. *Feminist Review, 122*(1), 32–48.

Fletcher, R. (1995). Silences: Irish women and abortion. *Feminist Review, 50*(1), 44–66.

Fletcher, R. (1998). "The pro-life" absolutes, feminist challenges: The fundamentalist narrative of Irish abortion law 1986–1992. *Osgoode Hall Law Journal, 36*(1), 1–62.

Fletcher, R. (2001). Post-colonial fragments: Representations of abortion in Irish law and politics. *Journal of Law and Society, 28*(4), 568–589.

Fletcher, R. (2018). #RepealingThe8th: Translating travesty, global conversation, and the Irish abortion referendum. *Feminist Legal Studies, 26*(3), 233–259.

Fletcher, R. (2020). Cheeky witnessing. *Feminist Review, 124,* 24–141.

Flynn, T. (2015). You don't talk about abortion in Ireland. But I have to. *Irish Times.* Available at http://www.irishtimes.com/life-and-style/people/tara-flynn-you-don-t-talk-about-abortion-in-ireland-but-i-have-to-1.2344617 (accessed 1 June 2019).

Fogarty, M., Ryan, L., & Lee, J. (Eds.). (1984). *Irish values and attitudes: The Irish report of the European Value Systems Study.* Dublin: Dominican Publications.

Foley, D. (2019). "Too many children?": Family planning and *Humanae Vitae* in Dublin, 1960–1972. *Irish Economic and Social History, 46*(1), 142–160.

Ford, C. (2015). #ShoutYourAbortion: If you've had an abortion, you have nothing to apologise for. *Daily Life.* Available at http://www.dailylife.com.au/news-and-views/dl-opinion/shoutyourabortion-if-youve-had-an-abortion-you-have-nothing-to-apologise-for-20150921-gjrmc6.html (accessed 1 July 2019).

Fox, M., & Murphy, T. (1992). Irish abortion: Seeking refuge in a jurisprudence of doubt and delegation. *Journal of Law and Society, 19*(4), 454–466.

Francke, L. B. (1978). *The ambivalence of abortion.* New York: Penguin Books.

Francome, C. (1992). Irish women who seek abortions in England. *Family Planning Perspectives, 24*(6), 265–268.

Freedman, L., & Weitz, T. A. (2012). The politics of motherhood meets the politics of poverty. *Contemporary Sociology, 20*(1), 36–42.

Gentleman, A. (2015). How heartbreak led Helen and Graham Lenihen to campaign for abortion in Ireland. *Guardian.* Available at https://www.theguardian.com/world/2015/oct/19/graham-helen-linehan-ireland-abortion-amnesty-international (accessed 1 June 2019).

Gilmartin, M., & White, A. (2011). Interrogating medical tourism: Ireland, abortion, and mobility rights. *Signs: Journal of Women in Culture and Society, 36*(2), 275–280.

Ginsburg, F., & Rapp, R. (1995). *Conceiving the new world order: The global politics of reproduction.* Berkeley: University of California Press.

Girvin, B. (2008). Contraception, moral panic and social change in Ireland, 1969–79. *Irish Political Studies, 23*(4), 555–576.

Girvin, B. (2018). An Irish solution to an Irish problem: Catholicism, contraception and change, 1922–1979. *Contemporary European History, 27*(1), 1–22.

Greene Foster, D. (2020). *The turnaway study: Ten years, a thousand women, and the consequences of having-or being denied-an abortion.* New York: ANSIRH Press.

Griffin, G., O'Connor, O., Smyth, A., & O'Connor, A. (2019). *It's a yes! How Together for Yes repealed the Eight and transformed Irish society.* Dublin: Orpen Press.

Guttmacher Institute. (2016). *Fact sheet: Abortion in the United States.* Available at https://www.guttmacher.org/sites/default/files/factsheet/fb_induced_abortion_3.pdf (accessed 22 Nov 2019).

Guttmacher Institute. (2019). *What the Trump administration's final regulatory changes mean for Title X.* Guttmacher Institute. Available at https://www.guttmacher.org/article/2019/03/what-trump-administrations-final-regulatory-changes-mean-title-x (accessed 31 May 2020).

Hadley, J. (1997). The "awfulisation" of abortion. *Choices, 26*(1), 7–8.

Hallgarten, L. (2018). Abortion narratives: Moving from statistics to stories. *The Lancet, 391*(10134), 1988–1989.

Hamilton, I. (2018). *The hashtag campaign saying 'Hear Me Out' about Ireland's abortion laws.* Mashable. Available at https://mashable.com/2018/05/21/hearmeout-campaign-irish-referendum/?europe=true (accessed 28 May 2020).

Harding, M. (2014). Irish abortion law: Legislating to stand still. *International Survey of Family Law, 20*(1), 201–226.

Health Act. (2018). *Health (Regulation of Termination of Pregnancy) Act 2018.* Dublin: Oireachtas.

Health Services Executive. (2013). *Final report: Investigation of incident 50278 from time of patient's self referral to hospital on 21st of October 2012 to the patient's death on 28th October 2012.* Dublin: HSE.

Healey, M. (2008). "I don't want to get into this, it's too controversial": How Irish women politicians conceptualise the abortion debate. In J. Schweppe (Ed.), *The unborn child, Article 40.3.3 and abortion in Ireland* (pp. 65–85). Dublin: Liffey Press.

Healy, G., Sheehan, B., & Whelan, N. (2015). *Ireland says yes: The inside story of how the vote for marriage equality was won.* Kildare: Merrion Press.

Herzog, D. (2011). *Sexuality in Europe: A twentieth-century history.* New York: Cambridge University Press.

Hesketh, T. (1990). *The second partitioning of Ireland? The abortion referendum of 1983.* Dublin: Brandsma Books.

Hill, M. (2003). *Women in Ireland: A century of change.* Belfast: Blackstaff.

Hilliard, B. (2000). Motherhood, sexuality and the Catholic Church. In P. Kennedy (Ed.), *Motherhood in Ireland* (pp. 120–145). Cork: Mercier Press.

Hilliard, B. (2003). The Catholic Church and married women's sexuality: Habitus change in late 20th century Ireland. *Irish Journal of Sociology, 12*(2), 28–49.

Hogan, C. (2019). Why Ireland's battle over abortion is far from over. *Guardian.* Available at https://www.theguardian.com/lifeandstyle/2019/oct/03/why-irelands-battle-over-abortion-is-far-from-over-anti-abortionists (accessed 21 Nov 2019).

Hogan, C. (2020). *Republic of Shame: Stories from Ireland's institutions for fallen women.* Dublin: Penguin Ireland.

Holland, K. (2013). *Savita: The tragedy that shook a nation.* Dublin: Transworld Ireland.

Holland, K. (2018). Savita Halappanavar's parents "really, really happy" after abortion vote. *Irish Times.* Available at https://www.irishtimes.com/news/social-affairs/savita-halappanavar-s-parents-really-really-happy-after-abortion-vote-1.3509839 (accessed 28 May 2020).

Holohan, C. (2018). *Reframing Irish youth in the sixties.* Liverpool: Liverpool University Press.

Hug, C. (1999). *The politics of sexual morality in Ireland.* Basingstoke: Palgrave Macmillan.

Hyland, P. (2012). Youth Defence under investigation over use of image in anti-abortion campaign. *The Journal.* Available at https://www.thejournal.ie/youth-defence-abortion-image-investigation-533369-Jul2012/ (accessed 28 May 2020).

Ingle, R. (2015). Why I need to tell my abortion story. *Irish Times.* Available at http://www.irishtimes.com/life-and-style/people/r%C3%B3is%C3%ADn-ingle-why-ineed-to-tell-my-abortion-story-1.2348822 (accessed 27 May 2019).

Inglis, T. (1997). Foucault, Bourdieu, and the field of Irish sexuality. *Irish Journal of Sociology, 6*(1), 5–28.

Inglis, T. (1998a). *Moral monopoly: The rise and fall of the Catholic church in modern Ireland.* Dublin: University College Dublin.

Inglis, T. (1998b). *Lessons in Irish sexuality.* Dublin: University College Dublin Press.

Inglis, T. (1998c). From sexual repression to liberation? In M. Pellion & E. Slater (Eds.), *Encounters with modern Ireland* (pp. 121–142). Dublin: Institute of Public Administration.

Inglis, T. (2005). Origins and legacies of Irish prudery: Sexuality and social control in modern Ireland. *Éire-Ireland, 40*(2), 9–37.

Inglis, T. (2014). *Meanings of life in contemporary Ireland: Webs of significance.* London: Palgrave Macmillan.

Irish Examiner. (2018). Taoiseach: Yes in abortion referendum would remove legacy of shame to women. *Irish Examiner*. Available at https://www.irishe xaminer.com/breakingnews/ireland/taoiseach-yes-in-abortion-referendum-would-remove-legacy-of-shame-to-women-844919.html (accessed 28 May 2020).

Irish Times. (2018a). Safe, legal and rare: Full text of Taoiseach's abortion speech. *Irish Times*. Available at https://www.irishtimes.com/news/social-affairs/safe-legal-and-rare-full-text-of-taoiseach-s-abortion-speech-1.3373468 (accessed 9 June 2019).

Irish Times. (2018b). Abortion and me: Share your story. *Irish Times*. Available at https://www.irishtimes.com/life-and-style/health-family/abortion-and-me-share-your-story-1.3484457 (accessed 1 June 2019).

Jackson, P. (1987). Outside the jurisdiction: Irishwomen seeking abortion. In C. Curtin, P. Jackson, & B. Connor (Eds.), *Gender in Irish society* (pp. 203–223). Galway: Galway University Press.

Joyce, T. J., Henshaw, S. K., Dennis, A., Finer, L. B., & Blanchard, K. (2009). *The impact of state mandatory counseling and waiting period laws on abortion: A literature review*. New York: Guttmacher Institute.

Kasstan, B., & Crook, S. (2018). Reproductive rebellions in Britain and the Republic of Ireland: Contemporary and past abortion activism and alternative sites of care. *Feminist Encounters: A Journal of Critical Studies in Culture and Politics, 2*(2), 1–16.

Katz, J., & Tirone, V. (2015). From the agency line to the picket line: Neoliberal ideals, sexual realities, and arguments about abortion in the US. *Sex Roles, 73*(8), 311–318.

Kelly, C. (2016). TwoWomenTravel should be—170,000 women travel. *Irish Independent*. Available at https://www.independent.ie/opinion/column ists/dr-ciara-kelly-twowomentravel-170000-women-travel-34998798.html (accessed 1 Apr 2019).

Kelly, F. (2018a, May 25). Yes vote shows overwhelming desire for change that nobody foresaw. *Irish Times*. Available at https://www.irishtimes.com/news/ireland/irish-news/yes-vote-shows-overwhelming-desire-for-change-that-nobody-foresaw-1.3508879 (accessed 25 May 2020).

Kelly, F. (2018b). Peadar Tóibín suspended from Sinn Féin over abortion law vote. *Irish Times*. Available at https://www.irishtimes.com/news/politics/peadar-t%C3%B3ib%C3%ADn-suspended-from-sinn-f%C3%A9in-over-abortion-law-vote-1.3682771.html (accessed 28 May 2020).

Kelly, K. (2014). The spread of "post abortion syndrome" as social diagnosis. *Social Science & Medicine, 102*, 18–25.

Kelly, L. (2020). The contraceptive pill in Ireland c.1964–79: Activism, women and patient-doctor relationships. *Medical History, 64*(2), 195–218.

Kennedy, F. (2001). *Cottage to crèche: Family change in Ireland*. Dublin: The Institute of Public Administration.

Kennedy, J. (2013). Youth Defence billboard posters not covered by advertising standards. *Irish Times*. Available at https://www.irishtimes.com/news/youth-defence-billboard-posters-not-covered-by-advertising-standards-1.954324 (accessed 28 May 2020).

Kimport, K. (2012). (Mis)understanding abortion regret. *Symbolic Interaction, 35*(2), 105–122.

Kitchin, R., & Lysaght, K. (2004). Sexual citizenship in Belfast, Northern Ireland. *Gender, Place & Culture, 11*, 83–103.

Kligman, G. (1998). *The politics of duplicity: Controlling reproduction in Ceausecu's Romania*. Berkeley: University of California Press.

Kumar, A. (2013). Everything is not abortion stigma. *Women's Health Issues, 23*(6), 329–331.

Kumar, A., Hessini, L., & Mitchell, E. M. H. (2009). Conceptualising abortion stigma. *Culture, Health and Sexuality, 11*(6), 625–639.

Larkin, L. (2018). "I went number after Mullens' ignorant comment". *The Herald*. Available at https://www.herald.ie/news/i-went-numb-after-mullens-ignorant-comment-long-36944277.html (accessed 28 May 2020).

Leahy, P. (2019). Aontú making a place for itself in Irish politics, says Toibin. *Irish Times*. Available at https://www.irishtimes.com/news/politics/aont%C3%BA-making-a-place-for-itself-in-irish-politics-says-t%C3%B3ib%C3%ADn-1.3894746 (accessed 21 Nov 2019).

Lee, E. (2003). *Abortion, motherhood and mental health*. New York: Aldine de Gruyter.

Lee, E. (2017). Constructing abortion as a social problem: Sex selection and the British abortion debate. *Feminism and Psychology, 27*(2), 15–33.

Lentin, R. (2013). A woman died: Abortion and the politics of birth in Ireland. *Feminist Review, 105*, 130–136.

Loughlin, E., & O'Cionnaith, F. (2018). How they did it: Behind-the-scenes of how the Eighth was repealed. *Irish Examiner*. Available at https://www.irishexaminer.com/breakingnews/views/analysis/how-they-did-it-behind-the-scenes-of-how-the-eighth-was-repealed-846478.html (accessed 4 May 2019).

Lowe, P. (2016). *Reproductive health and maternal sacrifice: Women, choice and responsibility*. London: Palgrave Macmillan.

Lowe, P., & Page, S. J. (2018). "On the wet side of the womb": The construction of mothers in anti-abortion activism in England and Wales. *European Journal of Women's Studies, 26*(2), 165–180.

Ludlow, J. (2008). The things we cannot say: Witnessing the traumatization of abortion in the United States. *Women Studies Quarterly, 36*(1), 28–41.

Ludlow, J. (2012). Love and goodness: Toward a new abortion politics. *Feminist Studies, 38*(2), 474–483.

Luibheid, E. (2013). *Pregnant on arrival: Making the illegal immigrant*. St Paul: University of Minnesota Press.

Lupton, D. (2013). *The social worlds of the unborn*. London: Palgrave Macmillan.

Maguire, M. J. (2001). The changing face of Catholic Ireland: Conservatism and liberalism in the Ann Lovett and Kerry Babies scandals. *Feminist Studies, 27*(2), 335–358.

Major, B., Appelbaum, M., Beckman, L., Dutton, M. A., Russo, N. F., & West, C. (2009). Abortion and mental health: Evaluating the evidence. *American Psychologist, 64*(9), 863–890.

Martin, G. (2015). *Understanding social movements*. London: Routledge.

Martin, L. A., Hassinger, J. A., Debbink, M., & Harris, L. H. (2017). Dangertalk: Voices of abortion providers. *Social Science & Medicine, 18*(4), 75–83.

McAuliffe, M. (2009). Irish histories: Gender, women and sexualities. In M. McAuliffe, K. O'Donnell, & L. Lane (Eds.), *Palgrave advances in Irish history* (pp. 191–221). New York: Palgrave Macmillan.

McAvoy, S. (1999). The regulation of sexuality in the Irish Free State. In E. Malcom & G. Jones (Eds.), *Medicine, disease and the state in Ireland, 1650–1940* (pp. 253–266). Cork: Cork University Press.

McAvoy, S. (2004). Before Cadden: Abortion in mid-twentieth-century Ireland. In D. Keogh, F. O'Shea, & C. Quinlan (Eds.), *The lost decade: Ireland in the 1950s* (pp. 147–163). Cork: Cork University Press.

McAvoy, S. (2008). From anti-amendment campaigns to demanding reproductive justice: The changing landscape of abortion rights activism in Ireland, 1983–2008. In J. Schweppe (Ed.), *The unborn child, Article 40.3.3 and abortion in Ireland* (pp. 15–47). Dublin: Liffey Press.

McAvoy, S. (2012a). Its effect on public morality is vicious in the extreme: Defining birth control as obscene and unethical, 1926–32. In E. Farrell (Ed.), *She said she was in the family way: Pregnancy and infancy in modern Ireland* (pp. 35–52). London: Institute of Historical Research.

McAvoy, S. (2012b). A perpetual nightmare: Women, fertility control and the Irish state: The 1935 ban on contraceptives. In M. Preston & M. Ó hÓgartaigh (Eds.), *Gender and medicine in Ireland 1700–1950* (pp. 189–202). Syracuse: Syracuse University Press.

McCafferty, N. (1985). *A woman to blame: The Kerry Babies Case*. Dublin: Attic Press.

McCarthy, J. (2016). Reproductive justice in Ireland: A feminist analysis of the Neary and Halappanavar case. In M. Donnelly & C. Murray (Eds.), *Ethical and legal debates in Irish healthcare: Confronting complexities* (pp. 9–23). Manchester: Manchester University Press.

McCarthy, J. (2018). Landslide victory for Yes side in referendum. *RTE*. Available at https://www.rte.ie/news/eighth-amendment/2018/0526/966152-eighth-amendment-referendum/ (accessed 1 Nov 2018).

McCarthy, R. L. (2010). *Origins of the Magdalen laundries: An analytical history*. London: McFarland.

McDonald, H. (2014). Brain-dead pregnant woman's life support can be switched off, Irish court rules. *Guardian*. Available at https://www.theguardian.com/world/2014/dec/26/ireland-court-rules-brain-dead-pregnant-womans-life-support-switched-off (accessed 28 May 2020).

McDonald, N., Antosik-Parsons, K., Till, K. E., Callan, J., & Kearns, G. (2020). Campaigning for choice: Canvassing as feminist pedagogy in Dublin Bay North. In K. Browne & S. Calkin (Eds.), *After repeal: Rethinking abortion politics* (pp. 124–144). London: Zed Books.

McDonnell, K. (1984). *Not an easy choice: Re-examining abortion*. London: South End Press.

McDonnell, O., & Murphy, P. (2019). Mediating abortion politics in Ireland: Media framing of the death of Savita Halappanavar. *Critical Discourse Studies, 16*(1), 1–20.

McGarry, P. (2018, July 28). How *Humanae Vitae* crushed the hopes of millions of Catholics. *Irish Times*. Available at https://www.irishtimes.com/news/social-affairs/religion-and-beliefs/how-humanae-vitae-crushed-the-hopes-of-millions-of-catholics-1.3578547 (accessed 25 May 2020).

McGee, H. (2018). How the Yes and No side won and lost the abortion referendum. *Irish Times*. Available at https://www.irishtimes.com/news/politics/how-the-yes-and-no-sides-won-and-lost-the-abortion-referendum-1.3509924 (accessed 9 July 2019).

McGreevy, R. (2018). The Citizens Assembly—A canny move on the road to repeal. *Irish Times*. Available at https://www.irishtimes.com/news/ireland/irish-news/the-citizens-assembly-a-canny-move-on-the-road-to-repeal-1.3510373 (accessed 29 May 2020).

McShane, I. (2018). 'Thirty-sixth amendment to the Constitution exit poll 25th May, 2018', *RTÉ & Behaviour & Attitudes Exit Poll*. Dublin: Behaviour & Attitudes.

Millar, E. (2016). Mourned choices and grievable lives: The anti-abortion movement's influence in defining the abortion experience in Australia since the 1960s. *Gender & History, 28*(2), 501–519.

Millar, E. (2017). *Happy abortions: Our bodies in the era of choice*. London: Zed Books.

Millar, E. (2020). Abortion stigma as a social process. *Women's Studies International Forum, 78*(2), 1023–1028.

Moore, A. (2019). Minister backs exclusion zones as US anti-abortion groups target Ireland. *Irish Independent*. Available at https://www.independent.ie/

breaking-news/irish-news/minister-backs-exclusion-zones-as-us-antiabortion-groups-target-ireland-37826853.html (accessed 21 Nov 2019).

Muldowney, M. (2013). Breaking the silence on abortion: The 1983 referendum campaign. *History Ireland, 21*(2), 42–45.

Muldowney, M. (2015). Breaking the silence: Pro-choice activism in Ireland since 1983. In J. Redmond, S. Tiernan, S. McAvoy, & M. McAuliffe (Eds.), *Sexual politics in modern Ireland* (pp. 127–150). Dublin: Irish Academic Press.

Mullally, S. (2008). Abortion law: Rights discourse, dissent and reproductive autonomy. In J. Schweepe (Ed.), *The unborn child, Article 40.3.3 and abortion in Ireland: Twenty-five years of protection?* (pp. 213–245). Dublin: Liffey Press.

Mullally, U. (Ed.). (2018a). *Repeal the 8th*. Dublin: Penguin.

Mullally, U. (2018b). Young women already being written out of the story of repeal. *Irish Times*. Available at https://www.irishtimes.com/opinion/una-mullally-young-women-already-being-written-out-of-the-story-of-repeal-1.3516216 (accessed 28 May 2020).

Murray, C. (2016). The protection of life during Pregnancy Act 2013: Suicide, dignity and the Irish discourse on abortion. *Social and Legal Studies, 25*(6), 667–698.

National Women's Council of Ireland. (2012). *Working to improve women's lives: Annual report 2012*. Dublin: NWCI.

Neville, S. (2018). People have been leaving flowers and notes at the Savita mural in Dublin. *Irish Examiner*. Available at https://www.irishexaminer.com/breakingnews/discover/people-have-been-leaving-flowers-and-notes-at-the-savita-mural-in-dublin-845251.html (accessed 28 May 2020).

Ní Aodha, G. (2018). Savita mural artist: "I've been painting a long time, I've never seen a reaction like that before". *The Journal*. https://www.thejournal.ie/savita-mural-artist-4044389-May2018/ (accessed 28 May 2020).

O'Brien, J., & Armstrong, K. (2018). It's a big Yes: Stunning victory officially confirmed as 66.4pc vote to reform Ireland's restrictive abortion laws. *Irish Independent*. Available at https://www.independent.ie/irish-news/abortion-referendum/its-a-big-yes-stunning-victory-officially-confirmed-as-66-4pc-vote-to-reform-irelands-restrictive-abortion-laws-36949114.html (accessed 7 May 2019).

O'Carroll, S. (2012, February 6). Twenty years on: A timeline of the X case. *The Journal*. Available at https://www.thejournal.ie/twenty-years-on-a-timeline-of-the-x-case-347359-Feb2012/ (accessed 26 May 2020).

O'Carroll, S. (2018). Savita Halappanavar: Her tragic death and how she became part of Ireland's abortion debate. *The Journal*. Available at https://www.thejournal.ie/eighth-amendment-4-3977441-Apr2018/ (accessed 22 June 2018).

O'Connor, A. (1992). Abortion: Myths and realities from the Irish Folk Tradition. In A. Smyth (Ed.), *The Abortion Papers: Ireland* (pp. 57–65). Dublin: Attic Press.

O'Reilly, E. (1997). *Masterminds of the right*. Cork: Cork University Press.

O'Sullivan, E., & O'Donnell, I. (2012). *Coercive confinement in Ireland: Patients, prisoners and penitents*. Manchester: Manchester University Press.

O'Toole, E. (2016). Abortion in Ireland: "Silence is breaking 12 hearts a day". *Guardian*. Available at https://www.theguardian.com/lifeandstyle/2016/aug/29/abortion-in-ireland-two-women-travel (accessed 26 May 2020).

O'Toole, F. (2003). The ugly politics of the womb. *Irish Times*. Available at https://www.irishtimes.com/opinion/the-ugly-politics-of-the-womb-1.368580 (accessed 25 May 2020).

Oaks, L. (2002). "Abortion is part of the Irish experience, it is part of what we are": The transformation of public discourse on Irish abortion policy. *Women's Studies International Forum, 25*(3), 315–333.

Petchesky, R. (1987). Fetal images: The power of visual culture in the politics of reproduction. *Feminist Studies, 13*(1), 263–292.

Plummer, K. (2010). Generational sexualities, subterranean traditions, and the hauntings of the sexual world: Some preliminary remarks. *Symbolic Interaction, 33*(2), 163–190.

Polletta, F. (2002). *Freedom is an endless meeting: Democracy in American social movements*. Chicago: University of Chicago Press.

Polletta, F. (2006). *It was like a fever: Storytelling in protest and politics*. Chicago: University of Chicago Press.

Polletta, F., Ching, P., Chen, B., Gharrity Gardner, B., & Motes, A. (2011). The sociology of storytelling. *Annual Review of Sociology, 37*(1), 109–130.

Pollitt, K. (2014). *Pro: Reclaiming abortion rights*. New York: Picador.

Porter, E. (1996). Culture, community and responsibilities: Abortion in Ireland. *Sociology, 30*(2), 279–298.

Power, J. (2018). Bishops "dismayed" at voices of abortion opponents being ignored. *Irish Times*. Available at https://www.irishtimes.com/news/politics/bishops-dismayed-at-voices-of-abortion-opponents-being-ignored-1.3722429.html (accessed 28 May 2020).

Purcell, C. (2015). The Sociology of women's abortion experiences: Recent research and future directions. *Sociology Compass, 9*(7), 585–596.

Quesney, A. (2015). Speaking up! Speaking out! Abortion in Ireland, exploring women's voices and contemporary abortion rights activism. In A. Quilty, S. Kennedy, & C. Conlon (Eds.), *The abortion papers Ireland: Volume 2* (pp. 150–164). Cork: Cork University Press, Cork.

Randall, V. (1992). Irish abortion politics: A comparative perspective. *The Canadian Journal of Irish Studies, 18*(2), 107–116.

Rattigan, C. (2008). "Crimes of passion of the worst character": Abortion cases and gender in Ireland, 1925–1950. In M. Gialanella Valiulis (Ed.), *Gender and power in Ireland* (pp. 115–140). Dublin: Irish Academic Press.

Rattigan, C. (2012). *What else could I do? Single mothers and infanticide, Ireland 1900–1950.* Dublin: Irish Academic Press.

Reinharz, S., & Davidman, L. (1992). *Feminist methods in social research.* New York: Oxford University Press.

Rocca, C., Kimport, K., Roberts, S. C. M., Gould, H., Neuhaus, J., & Foster, D. G. (2015). Decision rightness and emotional responses to abortion in the United States: A longitudinal study. *PLOS ONE, 10*(7), e0128832.

Rose, R. S. (1978). Induced abortion in the Republic of Ireland. *British Journal of Criminology, 18*(3), 253–254.

Rossiter, A. (2009). *Ireland's hidden diaspora: The abortion trail and the making of a London-Irish underground.* London: IASC Publishing.

RTE. (2012). Rallies held around Ireland in memory of Savita Halappanavar. *RTE.* Available at https://www.rte.ie/news/2012/1117/346029-vigils-in-dublin-galway-for-savita-halappanavar/ (accessed 11 Jan 2019).

RTE. (2013). Midwife confirms she told Savita Halappanavar Ireland a "Catholic country". *RTE.* Available at https://www.rte.ie/news/health/2013/0410/380613-savita-halappanavar-inquest/ (accessed 1 June 2019).

RTE. (2018). RTE exit poll on eighth amendment projects: Yes 69.4% no 30.4%. Available at https://www.rte.ie/news/2018/0525/965899-eighth-amendment/ (accessd on 12 May 2020).

RTE. (2019, April 17). Together for Yes co-directors make Time 100 list. *RTE.* Available at https://www.rte.ie/news/ireland/2019/0417/1043182-griffin-smyth-time-list/ (accessed 26 May 2020).

Ryan, L. (2007). "A decent girl well worth helping": Women, migration and unwanted pregnancy. In L. Harte & Y. Whelan (Eds.), *Ireland beyond boundaries: Mapping Irish Studies in the twenty-first century* (pp. 135–153). Dublin: Pluto Press.

Ryan, P. (2017, October 15). Varadkar defends comments on UK abortion journeys. *Independent.* Available at https://www.independent.ie/irish-news/politics/varadkar-defends-comments-on-uk-abortion-journeys-36227952.html (accessed 26 May 2020).

Redmond, S. (2018). *It's been two months now.* Feminist Ire. Available at https://feministire.com/2018/07/27/its-been-two-months-now/ (accessed 28 May 2020).

Reuters. (2019). *Tens of thousands march for ban on abortion in Slovakia.* Reuters.com. Available at https://www.reuters.com/article/us-slovakia-abortion/tens-of-thousands-march-for-ban-on-abortions-in-slovakia-idUSKBN1W70I5 (accessed 22 Nov 2019).

Rivetti, P. (2019). Race, identity, and the state after the Irish abortion referendum. *Feminist Review, 122,* 121–188.

Ruane, M. (2000). *The Irish journey: Women's stories of abortion.* Dublin: Irish Family Planning Association.

Ryan Report. (2009). *The report of the commission to inquire into child abuse.* Dublin: Department of Children and Youth Affairs.

Sanger, C. (2017). *About abortion: Terminating pregnancy in 21-st century America.* New York: Harvard University Press.

Schweppe, J. (2008). Introduction. In J. Schweppe (Ed.), *The unborn child, Article 40.3.3 and abortion in Ireland* (pp. 1–14). Dublin: Liffey Press.

Scriven, R. (2020). Placing the Catholic Church: The moral landscape of repealing the 8th. In K. Browne & S. Calkin (Eds.), *After repeal: Rethinking abortion politics* (pp. 191–204). London: Zed Books.

Share Your Abortion Story. (2013). Available at ShareYourAbortionStory.tumblr.com (accessed 29 May 2020).

Sheldon, S. (2016). How can a state control swallowing? The home use of abortion pills in Ireland. *Reproductive Health Matters, 24*(48), 90–101.

Sheldon, S. (2018). Empowerment and privacy? Home use of abortion pills in the Republic of Ireland. *Signs, 43*(4), 823–849.

Sheridan, K. (2018). Friday is about so much more than abortion. *Irish Times.* Available at https://www.irishtimes.com/opinion/kathy-sheridan-friday-is-about-so-much-more-than-abortion-1.3504515 (accessed 28 May 2020).

Side, K. (2011). A B and C. versus Ireland: A new beginning to access legal abortion in the Republic of Ireland? *International Feminist Journal of Politics, 13*(3), 390–412.

Side, K. (2016). A geopolitics of migrant women, mobility and abortion access in the Republic of Ireland. *Gender, Place & Culture, 23*(12), 1788–1799.

Side, K. (2020). Abortion im/mobility: Spatial consequences in the Republic of Ireland. *Feminist Review, 124,* 15–31.

Siggins, L. (2016, April 11). RTE told us our abortion film lacked balance. *Irish Times.* Available at https://www.irishtimes.com/life-and-style/people/rt%C3%A9-told-us-our-abortion-film-lacked-balance-1.2602308 (accessed 26 May 2020).

Silverman, D. (2001). *Interpreting qualitative data: Methods for analysing talk, text and interaction.* New York: Thousand Oaks.

Sisson, G., & Kimport, K. (2014). Telling stories about abortion: Abortion-related plots in American film and television, 1916–2013. *Contraception, 89*(5), 413–418.

Smyth, A. (Ed.). (1992). *The abortion papers Ireland: Volume I.* Dublin: Attic Press.

Smyth, A. (1995). States of change: Reflections on Ireland in several uncertain parts. *Feminist Review, 50,* 24–43.

Smyth, A. (2018). The obvious explanations of how power is held and exercised over women are very basic. In U. Mullally (Ed.), *Repeal the 8th* (pp. 124–140). Dublin: Penguin.

Smyth, L. (1998). Narratives of Irishness and the problem of abortion: The X Case 1992. *Feminist Review, 60,* 61–83.

Smyth, L. (2005). *Abortion and nation.* New York: Routledge.

Smyth, L. (2015). Ireland's abortion ban: Honour, shame, and the possibility of a moral revolution. In A. Quilty, S. Kennedy, & C. Conlon (Eds.), *The abortion papers Ireland: Volume 2* (pp. 167–178). Cork: Cork University Press.

Solinger, R. (2005). *Pregnancy and power: A short history of reproductive politics in America.* New York: NYU Press.

Solinger, R. (2013). *Reproductive politics: What everyone needs to know.* New York: Oxford University Press.

Solomons, M. (1992). *Pro life? The Irish question.* Dublin: Lilliput Press.

Specia, M. (2018). How Savita Halappanavar's death spurred Ireland's abortion rights campaign. *New York Times.* Available at https://www.nytimes.com/2018/05/27/world/europe/savita-halappanavar-ireland-abortion.html (accessed 12 June 2019).

Speed, A. (1992). The struggle for reproductive rights: A brief history in its political context. In A. Smyth (Ed.), *The abortion papers* (pp. 85–98). Dublin: Attic Press.

Staunton, C. (2011). As easy as A, B and C: Will A, B and C v. Ireland be Ireland's wake-up call of abortion rights? *European Journal of Health Law, 18*(2), 205–219.

Stopper, A. (2005). *Mondays at Gaj's: The story of the Irish Women's Liberation Movement.* Dublin: Liffey Press.

Storyful. (2018). *Ireland's abortion referendum is a test case for democracy.* Storyful. Available at https://storyful.com/resources/blog/how-irelands-abortion-referendum-became-a-test-case-for-democracy-in-the-social-media-age/ (accessed 28 May 2020).

The X-ile Project. (2015). Available at www.x-ileproject.com (accessed 29 May 2020).

Thompson, I. (2018). *How Irish anti-abortion activists are drawing on Brexit and Trump campaigns to influence referendum.* Open Democracy. Available at https://www.opendemocracy.net/en/5050/irish-anti-abortion-campaigners-brexit-trump-data-companies/ (accessed 28 May 2020).

Thomsen, C. (2013). From refusing stigmatization toward celebration: New directions for reproductive justice activism. *Feminist Studies, 39*(1), 149–158.

Tobin, B. (2016). Marriage equality in Ireland: The politico-legal context. *International Journal of Law, Policy and the Family, 30*(2), 115–130.

Two Women Travel. (2016a, August 20). *boarding, it's chilly. @endakennyTD*. Twitter. Available at https://twitter.com/twowomentravel?lang=en (accessed 25 May 2020).

Two Women Travel. (2016b, August 20). *We stand in solidarity with all women exiled @EndaKennyTD, his predecessors, his apologists*. Twitter. Available at https://twitter.com/twowomentravel?lang=en (accessed 25 May 2020).

Two Women Travel. (2016c, August 20). *pretty ordinary sights, in a place away from home, can't say it's comforting, though @endakennyTD*. Twitter. Available at https://twitter.com/twowomentravel?lang=en (accessed 25 May 2020).

Two Women Travel. (2016d, August 21). *@endakennyTD forced by more Irish in waiting room*. Twitter. Available at https://twitter.com/twowomentravel?lang=en (accessed 25 May 2020).

Two Women Travel. (2016e, August 21). *@endakennytd all done and dusted, we won't get home for another 24hrs*. Twitter. Available at https://twitter.com/twowomentravel?lang=en (accessed 25 May 2020).

Two Women Travel. (2016f, August 21). *Not for the first or the last time a bleeding woman about to face a long treck home*. Twitter. Available at https://twitter.com/twowomentravel?lang=en (accessed 25 May 2020).

Two Women Travel. (2016g, August 21). *We are nearly home. Thanks to everyone for unreal support—with one glaring exception. @endakennyTD*. Twitter. Available at https://twitter.com/twowomentravel?lang=en (accessed 25 May 2020).

Two Women Travel. (2016h, August 21). *A series of waiting rooms, a sequence of tediums*. Twitter. Available at https://twitter.com/twowomentravel?lang=en (accessed 25 May 2020).

Wanrooij, B. P. F. (1999). Italy: Sexuality, morality and public authority. In F. X. Eder, L. A. Hall, & G. Hekma (Eds.), *Sexual cultures in Europe: National histories* (pp. 114–138). Manchester: Manchester University Press.

Waterson, J., & Duncan, P. (2018). Irish anti-abortion campaigners dodge Google's ad ban. *Guardian*. Available at https://www.theguardian.com/world/2018/may/24/irish-anti-abortion-campaigners-dodge-google-ad-ban (accessed 28 May 2020).

Weitz, T. A. (2010). Rethinking the mantra that abortion should be 'safe, legal, and rare'. *Journal of Women's History, 22*(3), 161–172.

Whelan, N. (2012). Decisive change in the abortion debate. *Irish Times*. Available at https://www.irishtimes.com/opinion/decisive-change-in-the-abortion-debate-1.553268 (accessed 7 June 2019).

Yates, R. (1961). *Revolutionary road*. New York: Little Brown.

INDEX

Printed by Printforce, the Netherlands